Chasing Away the Shadows
An Adoptee's Journey to Motherhood

by
Zara Phillips

 GATEWAY PRESS, INC.
Baltimore, MD   2004

Cover Photos by Jonathan Phillips
Cover Design by Sara Clareheart

Please direct all correspondence and book orders to:
Zara Music
PO Box 10601
Burbank, CA 91510-0601
www.zaramusic.com

Library of Congress Control Number 2004115368
ISBN 0-9762661-0-5

Published for the author by
Gateway Press, Inc.
1001 N. Calvert Street
Baltimore, MD 21202-3897

www.gatewaypress.com

Printed in the United States of America

DEDICATION

To Jonathan, Zachary, Kayla and Arden
with gratitude and more love
than I ever dreamed.

This book is especially for those
who have been adopted—

May you find your voice and never feel alone—
And for all people whose lives
have been touched by adoption.

CONTENTS

CONTENTS

ACKNOWLEDGEMENTS

I would like to acknowledge all the people who have helped me on my journey.

First, thank you to Jonathan for understanding and supporting me through this project, for your willingness to learn about adoption, for not leaving when I have been completely mad, and for comforting me through my grief and helping me heal my heart.

My editor, Jane Lawrence—I just knew you were the one! Thankyou-thankyou-thankyou for all your hard work and your patience and understanding and encouraging me and helping me to finish this book.

Thank you so much Marlou Russell, for helping me find my voice and introducing me to all the wealth of information there is on adoption and encouraging me to write about my experience.

I would like to thank Alison Larkin for being British, adopted, having babies at the same time as I, living in LA when you did, and for your humor and friendship.

Thank you to all the good witches: Lynne Oyama, Jeannette Ryan, Candace Calloway, Marion Mayer, Catherine Hunter, Suki Low. I strive to be like you all. Each of you has blessed me so much with your kindness, compassion, and helping me see that I am not so bad after all!

I would like to thank Julie Dresel for befriending me in LA and having babies at the same time as I and always being available. Our friendship means a lot to me.

Thank you to Dr. Fleiss, the best pediatrician in the world. You have helped me follow my heart on how to raise children and always make me feel like the best mother, even when I really haven't been! And to all the ladies in the office—what a wonderful place it is. Thank you.

Thank you to Dr. Bates and Dwight for allowing my babies' births to be how I wanted. I feel so fortunate to have had you both with me during those times.

Thank you to Gieselle Whitwell

For all my American friends:

Richard and Georgiana Thomas, were we supposed to meet or what?

Terry Rink, what a hairdresser!!!

Eliza Roberts, thanks for telling me so much about LA. What a source of information you are!

Mike and Sandy, for so much . . . our chats, friendship, and your love.

Greg Eichler, for your friendship and support over the years and, of course, your lovely wife, Marrianne.

Audrey Harris for your gentle firmness. You have helped me so much.

Katherine Kennedy for stepping in when most needed!

Thank you to all my new Burbankian friends:

Shelly, you rock!!!!

Penny and Gina, for your Englishness and encouragement.

To our babysitters, who have saved me (and the children) over and over: Stephanie we cannot manage without you!!!! Thankyou-thankyou!!! Gina, for stepping in. Icela, for all your work.

Thank you to Cathy O'Brien for walking the walk.

To sister adoptees:

Trish Lay and Seanna Marre.

Thank you to Sharon Ness, Mindy Stern, Diane Rivers, Marlou Russell, Adele Mills, and for all the mothers who shared their stories with me so long ago. Thank you for revealing to me that I am not alone.

Thank you to Mimi Janes and Karen Vedder from CUB for all your support over the years.

Thank you to Nancy Verrier for her tremendous insight and for writing "The Primal Wound," it helped me in so many ways. Thank you also for all your help.

I would like to thank Susan Mello Souza for all her encouragement and hard work in helping me bring this book to fruition.

My dear English friends, whom I love and miss so much (thank goodness for cheap telephone rates!):

Serena Jameson and Anita Nurse (the best-looking over-forty-year-olds I know!) Thank you for all the talks over the years and your love and friendship.

To Jimmy McCaffry and Terry Dove (for talking to me at that first meeting and for all the support you gave me over the years . . . for taking me bowling). I will never forget what you did for me.

Bald Paul for being bald and always around to listen and have fun with.

Jonse for those early days of dancing sober!

Fiona, for swearing constantly and making me laugh when I sooo wanted to cry.

To Wendy Meredith Selway and Kerry Hastings, who came with me on my search.

Thank you to Bob and Shirley Sharpe for your insight, love, and rude emails.

Thank you to Melanie Redmond for taking me to Italy after I found out my birthfather was Italian. That meant a lot to me. What fun we had!

Thank you to Anna Ickowitz for consistent love, advice, caring, and mothering. You have helped me tremendously through the years.

Thank you Jane Grant for being you. What a source of inspiration!

For my old friends who have stayed in touch:

Virginia Davie, for driving me around before I had wheels, David Strickland, for driving me away from school at lunchtime (and all the other stuff that cannot be printed!), and Zoe Strickland.

I would like to thank all The Mount School Girls .

Roberta Duke, for being my inseparable sister through childhood.

I would like to thank Nikki Gold for being adopted and for that day we took off school when we were fourteen. I couldn't have done it without you.

I would like to thank Bill Hanks for his kindness in sending me the original photos of Gracie Field's house where I was born. It meant so much to me and helped me fill that missing piece.

Ronnie Paris for songwriting then and now, and allowing me to cry at your house when things were hard between my birthmother and me.

For dear sweet Nina Sepal you will always be my other baby, no matter how old you are!!
I love you.

My dear friend and sister, Katie Lachter, who has listened to me since before we had words: No of course I didn't forget you!!!!! I love you. Thank you for your endless support, patience, and pulling my covers when I am lying through my teeth.

To my adoptive family - my mother, my father, and my brother, Grant, thank you for everything. I love you.

To my birth family with love - my birthmother, Pat, my sister, Roberta, and my brother, Orlando. And, to my birth father, wherever he may be.

INTRODUCTION

Writing this book has been a fascinating journey. As a whole, the experience has been truly cathartic. For a long time I wrote just for catharsis, not thinking much about who would read it, because if I did, I would want to start editing for fear of opening myself up to criticism and—even worse—hurting my family.

Initially, I planned to focus on how adoption had affected my experience of motherhood. When someone suggested that I include more of my life story to illuminate the developmental issues surrounding adoption, I found myself going back and forth. Debating what to add, what to say, and worried over how the people close to me would react. In retrospect, wanting to protect everyone was actually a very adoptee-like thing to do. (You may well ask why that is. I am still not sure exactly, but as a child I tried to protect my loved ones out of fear of abandonment. I am continually amazed that at the age of thirty-nine, that instinct is still an integral part of who I am.)

This book is merely my experience, a view of my life as an adoptee. It is not intended to tell the story of any other individual. I am not an expert on adoption nor do I pretend to know all the scientific background, medical facts, or statistics. I can only share my story, my feelings, for they are all I have. Not all adoptees will have had my experience—we are all different. Nevertheless, many of the issues I have had to confront and resolve will resonate with other adoptees.

For me, adoption is gazing in the mirror and having no idea whom you look like. It is staring and staring at your adoptive family, searching for a resemblance and finding none. It is looking as hard as you can at everyone you meet and grasping at anything that could give you a sense of connection—the same color hair perhaps, or similar eyes, and feeling your heart skip a beat when you think maybe you really do look like the man on TV, only to find out he's a chief of police somewhere in Bosnia and you know that your birth mother never traveled. It is staring at families when you are at a party or meeting your school friends' mothers for the first time and being absolutely floored at how much they look alike, and while you babble on about their astounding resemblance, they look at you as if you have gone quite mad.

Adoption is growing up with a gaping hole inside that you want so desperately to fill, but you have nothing to put into it— no conscious memory of your mother, no idea of how you came into the world. All you have is your imagination to fill the hole in any way it can—were you the product of a passionate love gone wrong? rape? incest? indifference? Your inner world is populated with shadows in a murky background, shadows that never emerge into the light.

Adoption is living a lie, telling your family you don't care who your biological parents were so as to protect their feelings, while all the time your eyes patrol the streets, just in case "she" happens to walk by. Adoption is a sadness so chronic you don't realize there's another way to feel, guilt for feeling that way, and confusion about why you were given up.

In adulthood, adoption is perhaps a search; one that takes years to complete or that never can be completed. Even with success, you may find that that terrible hole is not filled by your birth mother, that she does not connect with you, or show interest in the way you need it.

Nevertheless, I present this work in a spirit of great hope:

First, I hope that my book can be read by all people who have adopted children or are considering adoption. Adopting families and those contemplating adoption need to understand that their adopted child comes to them in a state of fresh bereavement. He (or she) has just lost not only his mother, but his name, his extended family, his heritage, and his genetic history. Just because these infants and children cannot articulate their loss doesn't mean they don't feel it. I believe that if adoptive parents can recognize their child's wound and not react as if the child lacks appreciation of its adoptive home or loyalty to its adoptive family, there is a greater chance for a close relationship. Listening and allowing and recognizing the grief and talking to the child about her loss is the matrix from which a bond can form between parent and child.

Please understand that we all, whether adopted or not, need to understand our heritage. To know the names of our parents is our birthright. Regardless of how much love, security, and opportunity you have to offer your adopted child, he will face unique emotional challenges as he grows up. *These are not your fault and do not reflect poorly on the quality of your parenting.* It is important that you not underestimate the impact of adoption and that you acknowledge your adopted child's feelings.

Until the past few years, adopting couples were told to treat the baby just like it was their own, that it would never know the difference. Yet these parents frequently found themselves with babies who didn't bond to them in the way they had hoped. No one understood that babies grieve the loss of their mothers that they are likely to have great difficulty in forming attachments to others, and are at high risk for addictive behavior.

Birth mothers were told to get on with their lives, that they would forget about their babies, that they were doing the right thing, and that they would be selfish to keep their babies. They were led to believe they would "get over it." Many women found that this was not possible. They were haunted their whole lives by their decisions, and some were never able to marry and have other children.

Second, I hope to educate the general public on the subject of adoption so we may all be aware enough to help adoptees and their adoptive families in the trials that adoption can bring.

Third and finally, I hope my story can help other adoptees who are struggling with anguish that they may not understand. Perhaps you may get something you need from this book and no longer feel alone in your pain. I am glad to say that today many studies have been done, and information is widely available. There are tremendous numbers of support groups, and people are beginning to tell the truth and heal their pain. My wish is that anyone involved in adoption will take advantage of all that is available to them. To that end, I have created a Resource Guide at the end of this book, listing publications that helped me, as well as organizations in the United States and Great Britain that address the issues of adoption.

In addition, the book contains sidebars with quotations from women who were raised in adoptive homes about the impact of adoption on their lives and, in turn, the impact of motherhood on their adoption issues. They kindly allowed me to interview them about these intimate and frequently painful matters, and I have given them pseudonyms to protect their privacy. Their generosity in sharing their stories is much appreciated.

PROLOGUE

One day, when I was about eight or nine years old, a friend asked me that ever-so-important question, "What do you want to be when you grow up?"

"An author," I replied promptly.

"A what?" she said, scrunching up her nose.

"An author, someone who writes books," I said proudly. "Actually, I am writing one now." I held up my red notebook to show her.

"Why would you want to do that?" she asked. "It's not homework."

As a child, I wrote stories all the time. I wrote assignments for school as well, but mainly I wrote at home in my room. I wanted to do it. I enjoyed it and I needed the escape from what I now recognize as the low-level depression that was always with me. I never realized then that thirty years later I would finally embark on the adventure of completing a book. Of course, as an eight-year-old, I had a very different idea of what its content would be. At that time, I wrote imaginary stories where the main character always triumphed over some disability. Maybe this is another of those stories. I'd like to think so.

CHAPTER ONE

Guy Fawkes Day 1605

On November 5, 1605, in London, England, a terrorist plot to blow up Parliament was discovered. Acting on a tip, soldiers caught a man named Guy Fawkes red-handed in a cellar under the Parliament building. He had fuses in his pockets and thirty-six barrels of gunpowder. Parliament was due to open later that day, and the plotters hoped to kill not only members of the House of Lords but King James I, Queen Anne, and Prince Henry. Their goal was to bring back Roman Catholicism as the state religion. Fawkes was tortured and executed along with other members of the gang.

Every year since then, on the fifth of November, for better or worse, people in England enjoy fireworks and light huge bonfires. Straw effigies of Guy Fawkes are dressed in old clothes and flung onto the bonfires. Celebrants watch him burn while eating baked potatoes and huddling around the fire to keep the November chill at bay. Brilliant fireworks displays, small private gatherings, and public celebrations make Guy Fawkes Day one that most people remember.

For me, November 5, 1964, is the day I decided to be born.

Guy Fawkes Day 1964

January 1964 was an exciting time in London. The music scene was busting wide open with the birth of the Beatles, the Rolling Stones, great fashion and, of course, free love. Amidst all this was a sixteen-year-old girl named Patricia who enjoyed being part of that scene. Pat loved going out at night to the clubs, ironing her long hair until it was straight—the fashion of the day—and wearing strands of tiny Indian bells, love beads, and miniskirts. She returned home in the wee hours with flowers in her hair, clutching the bells in her hand to silence them, lest they waken her parents or the neighbors. She also loved hanging out in a restaurant/club called Les Enfants des Terribles, "the terrible children," on her lunch break from her job as a shorthand typist. There she could not only eat and drink coffee but, also, dance with her friends before returning to work.

This was where Patricia, my birth mother, met Vittorio, my birth father. The club was situated in the heart of Soho on Wardour Street, which was surrounded by Italian restaurants and had become a meeting place for the many Italian nationals who had come to London in the sixties to work or to learn English. Vittorio worked as a waiter while studying English. He was about twenty-two years old and surely not intending to become a father so soon, especially with a girl he barely knew. He and Patricia had only a few dates, but she knows I was conceived after my birth father took her to see one of the "Carry On" movies, which were hugely popular at that time.

These movies were a series, each made with different titles and different scenarios but with the same ensemble of actors. The themes were things like "carry on nursing" or "carry on camping" and "carry on teacher." The stories were wacky and titillating, full of crude sexual innuendo, but as a child I loved them. When I found out after meeting Pat that I had been conceived after one of those movies, I wondered which one it was, as I had seen all of them.

Pat tells me she knew instantly that she was pregnant, but she was afraid to tell her parents. As sometimes happens when a life event is too overwhelming to assimilate, she pretended it wasn't happening. She remembers reading an article that gave information on how to tell if you were pregnant. It said that if you could squeeze a substance from your nipples called colostrum, you were pregnant. She tried it and colostrum oozed out. She was terrified. In 1964, nice, unwed Jewish girls did not get pregnant—especially by Italian men they barely knew. Pat told Vittorio she was pregnant, but he was not helpful. Once, he called Pat at home, but when her mother answered the phone Pat would not speak to him, a decision she later came to regret.

In today's atmosphere of tolerance, it is impossible for anyone who didn't live through those times to understand what a catastrophe an unplanned pregnancy was. It was looked upon as the worst thing a girl could do; it meant that she was morally degenerate and the shame that went with it was crushing. Unwed mothers were branded, as many birth mothers have told me, as "spoiled goods."

Patricia and her parents, Jews of Russian, Austrian, and Dutch background, lived in West London. They were not especially religious and never talked to her about God or spirituality. Particularly, they did not talk to their daughter about sex.

After Pat became pregnant, she stopped going out to the clubs. Either her parents didn't notice this dramatic shift or chose not to acknowledge it. Finally, her uncle observed a change in her body, and he spoke to her mother about his concern. Without discussion, her mother told Pat they were going to see the doctor. She says she just went along with it and once there, the truth came out: Pat was five months pregnant—too far along for an abortion.

Pat had thought of abortion all along. If she had known where to go, she would have had one without hesitation. Instead, she tried to ignore her situation, hoping that somehow it would just go away. Once her family found out, all decisions were made by them. Keeping the baby was never considered an option.

It was decided that Pat should go and live with her two uncles for the rest of her pregnancy and that nobody should be told the truth. Instead, Pat's brother and her friends were informed that she had been offered a job out of London and that she would be gone for a few months. She did, however, confide in a girlfriend with whom she used to go to the clubs.

The days in her uncles' flat were long and lonely. She says now that she can't believe she survived it or that she let her parents treat her that way. Nevertheless, her uncles and an aunt were very loving and supportive. To avoid neighborhood gossip, she was allowed to go outside only at night for fresh air and exercise. Pat spent most of her time reading and watching television while her uncles were at work. Sometimes her mother visited.

A few weeks before term, she was moved to a home for unwed mothers. The girls had various jobs—making beds and other light work. Each week, they were visited by a lady from social services who inquired about their health and answered questions about pregnancy. There was no real discussion of emotional needs or what it would mean to relinquish their babies, that the decision would forever change their lives. The mothers-to-be were told that giving up their babies was what was best for the child; that they would forget and be able to get on with their lives.

On November 4, Pat went into labor and was transferred to the local hospital, which had a separate building for childbirth. The Annex, as it was known, was situated on The Bishops Avenue, East Finchley, London.

This area of London was known for its beautiful and elaborate houses, where people with some wealth lived. The Annex had once belonged to a popular singer of the early twentieth century named Gracie Fields. I felt quite glad to learn I had arrived in this world on such an opulent street. I remember telling my friends, with my nose in the air, "Don't you know, I was born on The Bishops Avenue."

They replied, "Well, well," or "Oooh," and looked amused.

My birth mother remembers it as very elaborate, with a huge sweeping staircase. It was very unusual for a hospital to be surrounded by such wealth.

Pat's labor was long and difficult. At one point, she cried

out to the nurse on duty to help her. The nurse replied, "You made your bed and you can lie in it," and left her to labor alone until the head matron appeared sometime later. The delivery also was very hard. She hemorrhaged twice, but I finally arrived in the early morning hours of November 5, 1964. No one was there to celebrate my birth. Pat remembers hearing fireworks going off before midnight and wondering why London was celebrating so early. The hospital telephoned Pat's parents. Pat's brother answered the phone and, thinking that he was Pat's father, the nurse informed him of my arrival. Until then, he had known nothing. Even after finding out, though, he played along with the secret. He told no one he knew the truth about his sister until I reappeared twenty-four years later.

Apparently, there was a brief discussion about adopting me within the family, but that didn't happen. The matron of the hospital told Pat she knew of a German couple who would be interested in adopting me, but Pat's mother insisted the adoption be handled through proper channels.

After a week in the hospital, Pat was able to take me back to the mother-and-baby home. The following day, however, she developed an abscess and had to return to the hospital. When asked where her baby was, Pat had no answers. She didn't know why I hadn't accompanied her. While she was there—and without her knowledge—I was placed in foster care. When she returned to the mother-and-baby home a second time, I was gone. I remained with my foster parents until January 4, 1965, at which time I was legally adopted. I was two months old.

Living with Shadows

The people who were to become my father and mother had been born and raised in London; they were both Jewish. My mother's father was a watchmaker and jeweler who had fought in World War I and was a Home Guard in World War II. Both he and my grandmother died before I was born, but I am told they were very warm people. My adoptive mother told me often about how close they all were and how they enjoyed being together as a family. As I grew older, I found it fascinating that my mother should feel that way toward her parents; such connections were alien to me. I did not feel that way about anyone and felt guilty about it.

My parents spent their childhoods amidst the devastation of World War II. My father recalls sleeping on the underground train platform, crowded and uncomfortable, along with other Londoners fleeing the air raids above ground. My mother remembers walking home from school and seeing a plane they called a "doodlebug," which was actually a flying bomb. She thought it was following her, and was very frightened. She also recalls watching German and English planes dog fighting, which meant a midair duel. If they heard an air raid siren, they had to fall to the ground wherever they were.

My father was sent away to boarding school at age eight. The following year, the school was evacuated to Wales and, my father, at the grand old age of nine, decided he didn't like school anymore. He managed to get the train back to London and found his way home—to the shock and surprise of my grandmother.

My paternal grandmother was friendly with one of my mother's aunts. They both had sons the same age and would even get together for holidays at my father's grandmother's hotel on the coast. After my father went back to London to study for his law degree, his mother telephoned my mother's aunt. She told the aunt that my father was now at university. As fate would have it, the aunt's son, Reggie, was also at the same university, so they arranged for the two boys to get back in touch, as it had been many years since they had seen each other.

My mother met her cousin Reggie regularly at the university for lunch, and it was at one of those lunches that he brought along his friend to meet my mother. A couple of weeks later, there was a dance and Reggie asked if she would like to go.

"Only if you bring your friend," she replied.

Reggie then asked my father if he would like to attend the

dance.

"Only if you bring your cousin," he said, "because I don't like to dance and I won't go unless she is there."

Thus began their courtship.

Three years later, they became engaged. My father had finished his degree and had been articled (something like an apprenticeship) to a solicitor. My parents got married in September 1954, and were on honeymoon when they found out that my father had successfully passed his apprenticeship (similar to passing the bar exam in America) to become a solicitor.

The beginning of their married life was full of challenges and difficulty. They lived in a single room with only the barest necessities and received no financial assistance from either set of parents. Only ten weeks after the wedding, my mother's father died very suddenly. My mother, who had enjoyed an especially close relationship to him, was devastated. At the same time, my father was up for his turn at national service, which was compulsory in many European countries, at that time. Any day, he could be called up for as long as three years, so no one wanted to give him a job. This actually turned out to be the proverbial blessing in disguise, since it forced my father to open his own practice, which eventually became hugely successful. As his practice began to thrive and they were able to afford more comforts and amenities, I am sure my parents believed that the next stage would be to start their own family. My mother had always loved and wanted children, and although we have discussed it only briefly, I can imagine their disappointment and grief when they found out it was not possible.

They decided to adopt.

Their rabbi put them in touch with an adoption society in the heart of London. They had to produce various documents and explanations of why they wanted to have a child; they had to be interviewed in their home to make sure they would be acceptable parents. One requirement was photographs of not only themselves, but of their parents, too, along with descriptions of hair and eye color so that they could be matched with a baby that bore a general resemblance to them. Since they were Jewish, they were told they could adopt only a Jewish baby. My adoptive mother was upset and asked them why the baby had to be Jewish. The reply was, "Adopted children have many problems, and to give you a child of a different faith would only add to them." There was no guarantee that a baby would ever become available to them.

Happily, nine months after they applied, they were asked if they wanted to adopt my brother. They agreed straight away. When my brother was two-and-a-half, they received confirmation that there was a baby girl available. She was the last Jewish baby the adoption society had, and my parents were thrilled. This time, they waited eight months, and the main photograph the agency wanted to see was that of my brother—they wanted to make sure we would look similar.

In Judaism, it is the mother's line who determines whether the child is Jewish (paternity may be questionable, but maternity never is). The fact that my birth father was Italian and most likely Roman Catholic held no relevance for them: I had a Jewish mother and that was all that was important. They never felt it necessary to tell me about my Italian side. And so I joined their family. My adoption was finalized on the April 6, 1965, and my new birth certificate was registered with my new name.

My father continued to work hard in his practice. When I was thirteen years old, he became a district judge. He worked each day in the heart of London and continued to provide a very comfortable life for his family. He had little involvement in the raising of us children, which was quite common for that generation. He kept to himself, worked hard to pay for our education and, I believe, got all the information he wanted about my brother and me from my mother.

My father's father served in the armed forces in World War II, and I remember him at dinnertime saying to me, "Eat your greens. It'll make your hair grow!" I would always laugh, as my hair grew nearly to my waist. He was a kind man, but seemed to exist in the shadow of my grandmother, who had a large personality. She spoke without thinking, smoked constantly, and (so I am told) gambled his money whenever she had the opportunity. She was a great source of irritation to my grandfather just by being herself. I have many vivid memories of sitting around the table when they came to Sunday lunch, which happened most weekends.

Sunday was the only day of the week when we all sat opposite each other as a family and ate our food. The rest of the week, we sat in a row like birds on a fence along one side of our long green kitchen table in order to watch TV while we ate. Everyone had a great view except for me—I was on the far right end and couldn't see a thing except the dining-room table and chairs. Each time I asked to be moved or told them I couldn't see, they seemed annoyed. I could never understand why my brother got the best seat. I would sit quietly, but after a while I would feel a stirring from way low in my stomach, a mass of anger and frustration that felt ready to burst. These feelings were becoming all too familiar, but I didn't know how to manage or control them. I ate as fast as possible, which seemed to help me pass through the feelings.

On Sundays, though, the telly was turned off and we sat around the table. I had a great view of my grandparents. I would listen to my grandmother make a statement about someone and watch my grandfather start shrinking into his seat, muttering under his breath. "You *would* think that," he'd say, or would start tutting. There was lots of tutting whenever my grandmother spoke.

I knew she had upset my parents many times, but I was never told exactly what she had done. I did know, however, that she had never been forgiven nor was likely to be. She often angered my grandfather with her selfishness and outspoken ways, but I found her quite amusing. I also felt sorry for her, as I could tell that sometimes she was just making a joke. But nobody

9

found her funny and they would take any opportunity to show their irritation toward her.

As I grew into my teenage years and started smoking cigarettes, she was positively joyful. She would often say, "Zara, let's go and have a smoke," and off we'd go. She would offer cigarette after cigarette until I felt quite sick, and we would chat about this and that. I felt a connection with her, a fondness that still remains with me, although she passed away in March 2002.

My father's emotional distance caused me deep pain. My mother said it was because he was shy and that I had to accept that about him. But as a young girl, I took it extremely personally and felt a great rejection from him. Sometimes I would try to talk to him and he would just stare at the ground as if I weren't there. I couldn't understand why, and would feel the tears burning in my eyes and a tightening of my heart. The worst part, though, was the feeling of self-hatred that had begun to grow.

My mother worked with my father but was able to juggle being at home with us. She was a great homemaker and cook— also a great cab driver, as my brother and I would ask to be taken here and there. She was always available, and very involved in our lives. She did her best to please us and be a loving mother. She is a gregarious woman, who loves people and loves to talk. So different from my father.

Our family was complete and adoption was rarely mentioned.

CHAPTER TWO

Totteridge, England

I am sure that if my parents or brother were to write their own stories about our family, they would be very different from mine. After all, we all have different perspectives on life and what is important to us. I have read that if you stand a few people in front of a landscape or a painting they will all see something the others don't see.

Totteridge is a suburb in North London, and although it is not too far out from London itself, it is almost like living in the country. It had one long, winding, main road surrounded by grassy mounds and dirt tracks that mostly led to large old eighteenth-century houses. When I was a child, there was also a small farm where my mother often took me to buy fresh eggs and milk. I didn't understand why back then, since there was a Tesco supermarket just up the street!

Totteridge has an incredibly interesting history and is actually listed in *The Doomsday Book*,* which is England's earliest record of property listings. Once, for school, I had to do a project on the history of where I lived and learned that the name Totteridge is Anglo-Saxon, and that over the centuries it had been spelled at least eight different ways, including Taterig and Tattyridge, which I found quite amusing. I also learned that in 1946, a Bronze-Age chisel had been found in a street near our house, and that Julius Cesar passed through Totteridge in 54

---

* Written in 1086 by King William the Conqueror, *The Doomsday Book* was a survey of all the king's lands, including livestock, for the purpose of assessing taxes. It required two years to complete. Totteridge is listed at *Tattyrig.*

BCE. I loved knowing about the famous personalities who lived in the area, and would point out to visiting friends the house of the actor or talk show host. I also enjoyed the knowledge that Queen Elizabeth I had owned Totteridge Manor in 1562. In fact, anything with a plaque dating back so long ago held my immediate interest. I wanted to know the stories of what I called "the real people" behind it. I would imagine them walking the very streets and land that I stood on. Maybe I grasped onto others' history because of the void in my own.

Totteridge had one bus, the notorious 251, that never seemed to arrive on time. If you missed it, you could sit for up to an hour waiting for another. On the days when I decided it would be quicker to walk, it was certain that as soon as I was in between bus stops, a red 251 would whiz by. Sometimes I ran as fast as I could to catch it at the next stop, yelling to get the attention of the driver, but more often than not the driver never even slowed down. My journey up Totteridge Lane would have to be completed on foot. On those days, I looked lovingly and longingly at the old houses and wished that our family lived in one of them instead of the modern single-level bungalow that my parents proudly had designed and built for them in the sixties.

I had always wanted a house with stairs and various floors. Our house featured a long corridor, with doors on either side leading to our bedrooms. That corridor frightened me, especially when all the doors were shut. My dad would yell out to turn the light off before I had even got to my room. This became a constant argument, since the light switch was at one end of the corridor and my room was in the middle. How was I supposed to get to my room in the dark? I tried to explain it over and over again, but my dad had this fixation about turning off the lights so we wouldn't run up a huge bill. I tried various methods of getting to my room in the dark. Sometimes, by just feeling my way along the wall, with my heart beating anxiously and my hands convinced they were going to contact some slimy object—or worse, someone's body—before I got to my room. Upon finding my door and then the light switch, I would be so relieved that I would shut my door as quickly as possible without looking back into the dark void. The other option was to hear my dad yelling, "Turn off the light!" as I ran as fast as I could to my bedroom. I'd fling the door wide, turn on the light so that it spilled into the corridor, then run back and turn off the corridor light. It all depended on how I was feeling that particular evening.

The other inconvenience about our house was that the front door led straight into the TV room. You had to walk past my parents sitting on the sofa, which some of my friends found terrifying. My dad, who would only mutter a hello, was especially daunting. I would feel embarrassed by his quiet ways and get my friends through the corridor as quickly as possible, so we could get to my refuge - my bedroom.

The Good Adoptee

I stayed what they call the "good adoptee" for quite a while, keeping my feelings to myself, while watching my brother go through a difficult time. He would bring up the subject of adoption in anger and in tears. He would say all the stuff I wanted to say, like, "You are not my real mother," and "I want to find her." He showed his rage. But I saw how much it hurt our mother's feelings, so from an early age, it became my job to protect everyone. I felt I had to hide from them, that I, too, was angry, that I couldn't be honest. I thought I owed it to my mother not to behave like him, but that didn't last long.

My adopted brother and I often called each other names. I suppose most siblings do, but the word *bastard* was always loaded for us. "You're such a bastard!" I would say.

"But so are you," was his reply.

"But I am not a bastard anymore," I responded in defense.

"Once a bastard, always a bastard," he fired back.

Then I would run to my mother and ask if I really was a bastard, and she would say no, I wasn't, because I was now adopted, but I knew inside that adoption didn't take that label away. Back then, people still lived under the Victorian belief that if you were born a bastard, you were no good, stupid, not fit to live. Movies about earlier times just reinforced the judgment that you deserved very little if you were a "bastard child." Even at school as we learned about historical figures, it seemed essential to mention if they were bastards.

Naturally that was extremely confusing and conflicting for me. I felt drawn to that character or celebrity or writer that critics made sure to point out was a bastard, always feeling some identification with these people and was secretly glad to hear of their successes. It was a strange dichotomy: how could I tell anyone that I felt like a bastard, and understood these characters' struggles to succeed, their need for recognition? People believed that the word *adoption* took away the stigma, and along with it, the need to know your birth family.

Nevertheless, these consolations never worked, and I realize today that I believed all those subtle and not-so-subtle messages. I believed I was less intelligent than others, and that somehow my brain didn't work in the same way. It didn't help that I had an extremely hard time absorbing information—I could never pass examinations or finish homework unless it involved making up a story or a poem, and this added to my belief that I was indeed stupid, that I was different.

Then, of course, there was God and religion. Was I worthy of God's love? Was it my fault that I had been born this way? Had I done something dreadful in a past life? I knew one thing: I had better make sure God knew how grateful I was for being alive, and make sure to pray extra hard to make up for being a bastard so that I, too, could feel God's acceptance. This was tricky, because at the same time I was extremely angry with this loving God who made sure I was given up for adoption. I was convinced for a long while it was because I had been bad.

So *bastard* became great ammunition for my brother and me to taunt each other. Sometimes we laughed and other times we were extremely sensitive. That was our way of talking about adoption.

Imagination

As a child, I had always had the desire to express myself. At the age of eight, I began to write stories. They were mainly adventure fantasies, and as soon as one was finished, I would go to the kitchen and read it to my mother while she cooked. I also began to read more. I identified keenly with the Dickens character Oliver Twist, which confused me. After all, I had a mother hadn't I? I wasn't an orphan. I was also introduced to the story of Helen Keller, which I could get only from the library. I really wanted my own copy, but the book was no longer in print and the library wouldn't sell theirs to me. I checked it out many times, and subsequently found myself writing about disabilities and overcoming them. One of my stories was entered into a competition at school. I remember the teacher saying, "What an unusual topic for a girl of your age!"

Music was another great passion. Some days I couldn't wait to close the door to my bedroom and listen to a new record—usually a musical I had heard about. If I couldn't get the song book I would spend hours listening to the record, taking the needle off the disc after each line in order to write out the lyrics. Completing a single song could take half an hour, but once I had all the words, I could do the truly exhilarating part, the performance, where I played all the parts and sang all the songs. My only audience was my dolls and teddies, who always watched appreciatively as I lost myself in the emotion and beauty of words and music. Sometimes I pictured my birth mother sitting in a chair, smiling proudly at me.

I always had the feeling that I was being watched, like I was part of some experiment. I would find myself showing off to these "people," talking to them and feeling a certain comfort in their presence. Of course, I had no idea who *they* were, but I was convinced of their presence nonetheless.

Whenever a musical production was mounted at school, I rushed out to buy the record to learn all the parts. I did participate in these musicals, but to my great frustration, never had the lead part. My voice was so very deep for a little girl that it never appealed to the music teacher. She seemed to like pretty blonde girls with pure, high voices.

One day, an older girl heard my voice and told all her friends. After school, they surrounded me and demanded that I speak so they, too, could hear it. When they asked me to open my mouth, I pursed my lips as tight as I could for fear a sound would come out and they would make fun of me. I was never really sure if this deep voice of mine was a good thing or a curse. What did it mean to have a "sexy voice" anyway? I spent hour after hour singing alone in my bedroom, feeling the very depth of my emotion. It was strangely comforting. At those times, I felt a connection to the universe, to God. Yet when I finished singing, that connection was lost.

Hidden Truths

After school, practically every day, I hurried across the street to my girlfriends' house. Katie and Roberta and I had known each other since we were babies, and as we grew, we became inseparable. I loved being with them and playing with them. I so wanted to be their sister, and we were close enough to pretend we were. The connection between them was obvious, the similarities that made them family. I often felt great sadness because no matter how close we were, I wasn't their sister. When I left their house to go home in the evening, I felt an emptiness, a feeling that always took hold of me once I was alone.

When I was about twelve years old, I became aware that not all babies who were adopted were of the same religion or culture as their adoptive parents. That really bothered me. I couldn't believe that some children didn't know their origins, and became afraid that my parents were keeping something from me. A few days after first experiencing this awareness, I was standing in the kitchen with my mother. She had her back to me and was busy making supper. I mustered up all my courage and asked in a small voice, "Was my birth mother Jewish?"

My mother assured me that she was, and I said, "But how do you know? Was my birth father Jewish, too? Am I really Jewish?"

My mother said again, "Yes, you are Jewish," but she never turned to look at me. I knew then, staring at her back, that there was something she wasn't telling me. Her answer just didn't sit right in my soul, but at that time, I was still too scared to ask more for fear of upsetting her. I was to find out twelve years later that my birth father was Italian and that my parents had known this all along.

I was told it wasn't necessary to tell everyone I was adopted and never understood why, because I always wanted to tell people. One day at school, I was walking into my classroom when I heard some girls talking about me. I stopped quickly by the door so they couldn't see me and listened.

"She's adopted," I heard a girl say.

"Is she really?" said another voice.

"It is true—isn't it sad?" replied the first girl.

At that point, I made my grand entrance and the girls looked up. "I don't mind you knowing I am adopted. You can ask me any questions, or when you come over, you can talk to my mother. She knows more about it than me." I felt extremely important, so when my friends came over to my house, I told my mother they needed to talk to her about my adoption. I left my friends with Mum in the kitchen and went outside.

One afternoon, my brother and I stood at the front door with my mother and some of her friends. The husband gazed at me intently. "Who does she look like then? I think it's her dad." They looked at my tall, skinny, olive-skinned body and dark brown hair and then at my blonde adoptive mother and her shapely figure. "Yes," the man concluded, "she really looks like her dad." My mother readily agreed.

I stayed silent, but wanted so desperately to say, "I am adopted." The glance that came from my mother, though, made me feel it wouldn't be the right thing to say. I felt annoyed until my brother said, "It's pure coincidence, I can assure you." At that point, my brother and I looked at each other and cracked up laughing. The poor man didn't know what he had said, and Mother hurried him out the door.

Separation Anxiety

As a child, I could never fit in my bed, not because it was too small, but because there were so many teddies lined up next to me there was only a tiny space to squeeze in next to them. I loved my teddies and was very attached to them. I even remember writing nametags for them so when my babysitter came over she would know who they were when it was time to kiss them all goodnight.

I began to suffer silently from compulsive behavior. My teddies, for instance, all had to have partners so they wouldn't feel lonely, and I had to do everything twice. This became very annoying and would often delay my leaving the house or getting ready for the day. Some days, I found myself eating the same food twice so the food had company, or I walked endlessly back and forth across my room. Sometimes, I sat in my room and felt the walls closing in around me like I was being suffocated. Even at a young age I sensed that my behavior wasn't quite normal, but was unable to tell anyone what was going on inside.

When I was about twelve, I was invited to spend a week in Spain with a school friend and her family. I wanted very much to go, and thought I was grown up enough to go abroad. The day before we left, I stayed the night at their house, and lay awake in the dark gripped with that familiar fear I always had when I was away from home. I knew then I had made a dreadful mistake.

I spent the entire week in Spain in my bedroom. My friend and her parents tried to coax me out, but I would cry and shake and wait for my mother to call me from London. I needed the reassurance of her voice to calm what I can only describe as a rising panic. I wanted to go home, but was told by my hosts that I should stay and enjoy myself, that I would be okay.

I was embarrassed by my behavior and scared that my friend would tell everyone at school that I was a baby. But the fear crippled me, and I stayed in the bedroom. I wrote in my diary that I was adopted and was very lucky to have my family. That I loved them very much and I knew they loved me. "Being adopted hasn't affected me at all," I wrote. "I am so lucky to have been adopted and not put in an orphanage." I drew hearts around my family's names. When it was time to go back to London, I was so relieved, but when I got home, my brother made fun of me and my mother couldn't understand what was wrong with me. I was devastated.

Every time I stayed at someone's house, a parent would end up hearing me cry in the night and try to comfort me. I'd end up going home, ashamed that I wasn't able to stay away even a single night. I had no control over the feelings that surfaced—mainly intense fear. I believed that if I was away from my family, they would die, but as long as I could see them, everything would be okay. I never told anyone about these fears, believing that if I did, they would think me silly.

I have always loved babies and young children. Even as a child, if ever the opportunity arose to take care of a baby, I did it eagerly. One particular incident came back to me only recently. One Jewish holiday when I was ten or eleven, my family and I spent the day in synagogue. (Holidays were usually the only times we observed our religion.) I played all day with a small child. I had lots of energy and enjoyed being in charge. After the service the family asked if I would like to come back to their house and have dinner. My parents could collect me later or my hosts would drive me home. With my parent's permission, I readily agreed.

I felt quite shy, but the family was very welcoming. The mother was glowingly pregnant with her second child, and her husband very warm and loving. They both talked to me easily, including me in their conversations. When we sat down to dinner, some other family members joined us. I sat opposite the mother and watched the candles in the middle of the table and listened to the prayers and blessings. Once again, I noticed how happy and relaxed the mother was, and it made an impact on me.

Suddenly, I felt very sad, began to cry, and wanted to go home. I tried my best to hide my emotions, but the mother soon noticed. She took me out of the room and asked me very kindly and gently what was wrong. But I didn't know, I just wanted to go home, to get away from that terrible feeling I experienced whenever I was separated from my family.

CHAPTER THREE

Too Many Questions

In some ways I enjoyed the fact that I was adopted. It made me feel different from my friends, slightly romantic and mysterious, but I also felt I was missing out on something they had in their lives. I just didn't know what it was.

I had always thought about my birth mother but it wasn't until I started a new school and headed towards puberty that I began to feel the differences between my peers. I was in an all-girls school, and the relationships between my school mates were quite intense. I was becoming more aware of my body. Other girls would point out that I was skinny and had no breasts even at twelve years of age, and they wondered if I ever would. The girls talked about their bodies and their mothers' in comparison to themselves. "That is why I have fat thighs," my friend said. "I didn't stand a chance, it runs in my family. All the women have fat thighs."

Every day since I learned I was adopted in 1996 when my son was four, I stare at people who are biologically related to each other. It amazes me, people must think I am an idiot to be so floored that relatives look alike.

—Clara

I always laughed along with the other girls, unable though to participate in the conversation. In my silence, I wondered what I had in common with my birth mother. I would look at my friends and their siblings and felt the gap that separated me from them. I didn't fit in; after all, I wasn't the same as everyone else. I hadn't been born like them; actually I didn't know how I

21

had been born. I didn't have a birth story.

I wanted to know if my mother craved chocolate or oranges when she was pregnant, whether I was a week early or late, what I looked liked when I was born. When a school friend told me some detail of her birth, I was truly interested. Yet there was a huge space inside me that wouldn't fill up; I had nothing to go back to. I didn't have full-blood siblings with the same color hair and eyes. I didn't have a mother I could look at and say we looked alike.

I felt as though I had to lie and pretend that none of it mattered because I didn't want, at any cost, to hurt my adoptive parents or for them to not know how grateful I was that they had chosen me. Nor could I reveal to anyone the real belief I carried: that I must have been bad somewhere along the line or extremely ugly and defective because my mother had given me away and my friends' mothers hadn't.

I always had the feeling that I should be happy. I had, after all, everything: a nice house, clothes, I went to a good school, and I had many friends. Extreme guilt and confusion filled me because I wasn't happy. I wanted to believe the story of what other people thought of adoption; I was "special" because I had been "chosen" and was really wanted. When my mother read me the story of adoption, I tried so hard to be happy about it, not understanding why I didn't feel like others did.

I didn't want to hurt my mother by asking too many questions, so I began to protect my family from my real feelings. I was always scared of their reaction, their pain. Most importantly, I didn't want to be rejected.

Early Searching

In my class at school I had a good friend, Nikki, who was also adopted. We would talk about our situation and feelings and it was a great source of comfort and connection for me. When we were fourteen, we decided to take the day off from school and go up to Town to see what we could find out about our birth mothers.

We planned the day. Our parents dropped us off at school as they did each day but, instead of going into the school, we met outside, hiding behind the parked cars alongside the narrow, tree-lined street. Our school was a large Victorian house, nestled in greenery, with a small, dirt car park that stood halfway up a hill. The hill led down past a graveyard and to some sweet shops. We'd run through the graveyard and shimmy up a wall onto a concrete slab that levered us up onto the shop roof. From there, we found our way down between the buildings so we could go buy our sweets and cigarettes.

We chose to walk up the hill, where we wouldn't be visible from the school windows. The road wound past a triangular plot of grass with a medium-size pond. Alongside the pond lay a row of small attached houses that dated back to the eighteenth century. The tiny doors reminded us of how much smaller people had been back then. I thought they were wonderful and wanted so much to live in one of them.

We ran up the hill, ducking and diving behind parked cars. Once we were past the pond, we knew we were out of sight of the school and we had to worry only about teachers and pupils driving past and seeing us going in the opposite direction. We sneaked down a side street past the boys' school and onto a red bus that took us to a tube station. We hadn't thought to change clothes to make us less conspicuous, so we were still dressed in our school uniforms: shapeless brown skirts, pale blue shirts, navy sweaters, and our blazers with the school emblem embroidered on the front for all to see.

We headed to the heart of London to the Births and Deaths Office, in a building called Catherine House. We giggled a lot on the train, making jokes about who our birth mothers might be and became quite hysterical as only teenage girls can, causing a few raised eyebrows among our fellow passengers. We found Catherine House along the crowded streets and entered through a revolving door that led straight to the receptionist. Instantly we became quiet as our bravado faded in the bureaucratic atmosphere

I let Nikki do the talking. She always seemed to come across more grown up than I and this way, we would stand a better chance of being taken seriously. We told the receptionist we were doing a project for school, and she directed us to where the adoption birth certificates were located. The butterflies flitted in my stomach and my breathing grew shallow as we entered the room. "I feel sick," said Nikki. I quickly nodded in agreement.

We were both scared, but we went ahead, anyway, to look up our dates of birth. I found my adoption birth certificate easily. It gave only my adopted name and my adoptive parents' names—nothing else. I don't quite know what I expected to find, but I felt relief in part, because I could be sure that at least that part was true.

I heard Nikki from across the room. "Oh, my God!" She had found another girl with her exact name a year before her birthday. For a split second, she thought that she might be older than she was, but she soon found herself in the records. I could sense her relief.

By that point she seemed to be as ready as I was to leave. Once back on the street, we looked at each other. "Now what?" we wondered. We had picked up a pamphlet on obtaining adoption records that gave a phone number, and we decided to call the number to see what would happen.

We both huddled in the phone box and Nikki spoke in her grown-up way while I whispered what she should say. She wasn't on the phone long. The lady on the other end asked how old we were and suggested that we discuss this with our parents or wait a little while 'til we were older. Nikki put down the phone. We lingered in the phone box, our moods darkening.

"You hungry?" I asked at last.

"Yes," she replied. Off we went to have lunch.

Inner Emptiness

Growing up, I always had a heavy feeling in my heart, as though a claw with sharp talons was ripping at my insides. The result was constant sadness and a sinking feeling that would take me so fully at times that I felt sure I would never again surface into the light of day. The only time I enjoyed any relief from these feelings was when I was out in nature. There were occasions as a child of eight and nine when I would find myself laughing hysterically with my girl friends, feeling the wind and cold against my skin as we ran through the woods and fields near our home. In those moments, I found a lightness and freedom, an exhilaration that lifted me out of my normal darkness. But they were fleeting, and as soon as they were over, I was left once again with myself and the tightening claw.

I felt ugly most of the time, and didn't see myself as a normal, pretty little girl because inside I felt defective. Everyone else was better than I was. It was almost impossible to stop the self-hatred, the voice that repeated how silly I was when I made a mistake and the constant fear that people would reject me. The pain of rejection was to be avoided at any cost.

I fantasized a lot about my birth mother. I looked for her constantly on the streets; it was just part of what I did every day as an adoptee. Some people looked at trees or flowers; I looked at women's faces and wondered if I would recognize her or she me. Who was I? Where was I from? Was I English? Jewish? Really, what was the truth? On the other hand, I was scared to know the truth

I know my son looks "just like" me from others' comments, but because I was a different race from my adopters, I always thought I was hideously ugly.
—Adrian

because I also carried the belief common to adoptees that the mother who had given me away would never be interested in meeting me.

Sometimes I woke in the morning and imagined that this

was the day she would come and collect me. I would spend the whole day believing that she was about to arrive, peering out the window in hope of seeing her. I would fantasize about opening the front door, looking her straight in the eye, and deciding whether to invite her in or merely slamming the door in her face. Often I dreamed about her, but when it came time for me to look at her face, it was always blank.

I spent much of my time daydreaming and never really feeling connected with anyone. But secretly I was always waiting for the day that my birthmother would show up on my doorstep, apologizing and telling me there had been a terrible mistake.

My childhood was full of turbulent emotions, deep insecurities, and the terror of rejection. When I had arguments with my family or friends, I took everything so personally, so deeply, that I couldn't feel at peace until things had been resolved. I never wanted anyone to know the depths of my insecurity, nor could I really explain what was going on inside me. As I grew older, my difficulties grew bigger and more out of control.

I didn't know I was adopted until I was twenty-seven. I felt absolutely connected to my baby—he was the only thing I could feel connected to, even though I was still unaware of my adoption status. I didn't feel a connection to anyone nor did I resemble anyone [in my family]. Continuity seemed to be nonexistent.

—Martha

Paradoxically, feeling connected to anyone was incredibly frightening, yet connection was what I craved most. I tried many things to fill the inner emptiness, which felt as if it would devour me if I didn't anesthetize it in some way.

Information

My mother had a large suitcase filled with photographs of her parents and relatives. There were also letters that my parents wrote to each other, along with birthday cards dating back to before I was born and some from when my brother and I were small.

The soft brown leather was musty and scuffed with age, yet I loved that old suitcase. Even though the lock was broken, it still managed to contain everything. I often asked my mother if we could look through it. She was always happy to oblige and would stand on a step stool to reach up into her bedroom cupboard and take it down. After helping her lower it to the floor, we would then sit on the carpet and explore the contents.

I especially enjoyed finding anything having to do with my brother and me, such as early photos, birthday cards, or medical cards. I would ask my mother to identify everyone in the old black-and-white photos and to tell me how we were related. I always looked intently at those faces. I so wanted to feel connected to them, to really feel that they were my relatives, yet I always found myself wondering what my birth relatives looked like. I thought of the people in the photos as my mother's relatives.

I began to search my parents' belongings when they were away from home. As soon as they left the house, I would go through drawers and files to see what I could find, never consciously knowing what I was looking for. Perhaps they had a secret, maybe my parents weren't who they said they were. Maybe they were lying to me about my adoption, or things were a lot worse than they had told me. Worst of all, maybe I wasn't really adopted at all. I went through the same drawers time after time, convinced I had missed something. I never did find anything remarkable, but I never stopped trying. Even at night when I was meant to be in bed, I snooped around the house. I'd cram my ear to their bedroom door to try to hear what my parents were talking about: maybe they would mention me and reveal

My daughter is the only person I feel a total connection with in the whole world.

—Felicia

27

something I didn't know. I didn't realize, until years later, that it was information about myself I sought.

Childhood Bits

I knew very early that I was adopted. I have no memory of when I was actually told. I just remember a book. There was a roomful of babies lined up in their cribs, and a couple walked along, examining each one. There was one baby who didn't smile and was "far too serious" for them. They said he wasn't the right one, and they finally decided on a cute, happy, chubby baby, who was "exactly the kind of baby they wanted." The book invariably left me with a feeling of deep sadness. What, I wondered, happened to the serious baby? Who took *him* home to love?

My daughters were very excited for me when my records were opened. They came with me and were very supportive and emotional. They met my birth mother and have had contact with other family members, but they seem pretty neutral about it—it has not impacted them like [it has] me. They don't feel a deep connection.

—Janice

I could never express my depression to anyone. I often heard my family say, "Zara is just so moody." I became very angry when I heard that and also extremely depressed. It wasn't as though I liked being moody, yet I couldn't change it on my own and didn't know why.

I believe my parents wanted to think of us as their very own. My father has never mentioned adoption, and my mother talked about it only in answer to my questions—she never brought it up first. I longed for her to ask me how I felt about my birth mother, or to tell me that my birth mother had been pretty and good. I yearned for some scrap of history, for my own story. Their lack of acknowledgment made me furious and confused. Perhaps they were advised not to bring up the issue of adoption, but the message I got was that adoption was taboo. Consequently, I was extremely fearful of bringing up the subject. It took me days or weeks to work up my courage. I tried to ignore my pounding heart that beat faster and faster as I waited for an opportune moment to speak up. Then, for fear that my mother would be upset when she truly saw my desperation, I spoke in a small, off-hand voice which conveyed only cool interest. Her usual response was, "Your mother was young." I tried to look casual, when in reality I was concentrating hard so as not to miss one word of information.

When I was ten or eleven, I went through a phase of always making sure I came home with a present for everyone in the family—even the dog—when I went out shopping with my friends. My mother told me I didn't need to spend my pocket money on them, but I couldn't buy myself a gift unless I had something for my parents. I needed their approval, but mostly I needed to know they were going to keep me.

I felt very lonely and isolated. I truly believed that no one else felt like me, that I was different, that there was something wrong with me, that if people knew what was really going on they would lock me up. I became obsessed with books about serial killers and people with severe disabilities. I wanted to know how they dealt with their emotions, and was reassured that for all my feelings of insanity, at least I wasn't murdering people.

Acting Out

As I approached my teen years, my brother and I switched roles. He began to take drugs and appeared more reasonable (when in fact he was stoned), and I began to vent my anger, which increasingly deepened into rage. My Mother and I began to argue constantly until screaming and yelling at each other became part of the daily routine. My moods depended on whether or not I had something to look forward to, such as a party or a new boyfriend. But as soon as the party was over or the boyfriend was gone, I would spiral down once again into deep depression. Sometimes I snorted speed or cocaine to lift my mood. This enabled me to live with my mother somewhat free of conflict. The problem was I didn't know what I was angry about. All I knew was that I felt bad nearly all the time, really bad. If anyone noticed, they didn't know what to do. Neither did I.

Often I sought refuge in the local church and cemetery. I loved to walk among the seventeenth-century gravestones and read the inscriptions, then find their relatives buried nearby. I was drawn to the section where infants and children lay. Always worried that their headstones were too small and that they wouldn't be remembered. Inside the church, I experienced the peace and calm that only a place of prayer brings. As I reached my fourteenth year, the church became an essential place for me to go and have a much-needed cigarette, my first drug. I would tell my mother I was going for a run and would run to the church, where I could sit quietly hidden from the main street and feel my heart beat faster in anticipation of taking that first inhalation. With it came the instant relaxation of every fiber of my being. Aahhh, I felt so much better!

On the way home, I chewed gum, convinced that it would take away any lingering smell. If my mother guessed my secret vice, she never said a word. In fact, if my mother ever knew anything I was doing that wasn't in my best interest, she never said a word.

The picturesque local pub, The Orange Tree, had a pond with ducks and geese. There, I learned to fear those birds. Once, I took my friend's little brother to feed them. But he wouldn't let go of the bread, and the geese started chasing him. He wasn't much bigger than the geese, and as the long-necked birds lurched for his hand, I panicked. All I could think of was to shout at the geese and tell him to run. I was too scared for my own safety to rescue him.

When I was older, that pond became a source of great laughs. My friends and I would go to the pub on winter evenings. We were too young to go in, so we had to sit outside freezing, begging the older boys to get us a drink. My girlfriend, who had recently passed her driving test, managed to somehow reverse her car into the pond and got her wheels stuck. And, of course, there was always the threat of being thrown into the pond by some drunk.

After our nights at the pub, I often had to walk home. The old church and cemetery that I so loved in the daytime felt very different in the dark. No matter how much I tried to not look into the grounds, I couldn't help myself. I could swear I saw things moving among the headstones, and I'd end up running as fast as lightning down the little lane to the top of our street, where it was safe again. My parents didn't know I walked back from the pub so often. They thought my brother had taken me to the pub on the back of his motorcycle or dropped me at home. Usually he said, "Find your own way home, I'm busy." Then I would see some long-haired blonde jump on the back and ride off with him, her arms tight around his waist and him beaming like the Cheshire cat, revving the engine extra loud so everyone would turn to look at him.

I would roll my eyes in disgust and feel mad that she got to hold him by the waist. I was never allowed to—I could ride only with my hands hanging onto the bar behind me. Consequently, I never felt safe. As my brother took sharp turns, I saw the road inches from my face, and prayed to live. I had learned not to scream, since that made him really angry.

Grant

It is indeed strange to grow up with someone who is your brother when you both know that genetically you are not related at all. That you both have different parents and that there is a strong chance you have real siblings somewhere out in the world that look very much like yourself.

My relationship with Grant had a tremendous impact on my life. As a young boy, my brother was extremely withdrawn, staying in his room away from people as much as possible. I, on the other hand, had lots of friends and liked to socialize. As he grew to his teens, my brother changed a lot and began to make himself known by shaving his head and piercing his ear, which, at the time, was quite shocking.

I remember seeing Grant smoke marijuana for the first time. He allowed me into his room, a privilege I dared not refuse. I sat on the bed and watched attentively as he rolled a joint and smoked it. My response to watching him smoke was as if I had smoked it myself: I felt as though an electrical current rushed through my body. I was extremely scared, yet I was exhilarated too, by a rush of excitement and didn't know why. One thing I did know was that life was about to change, that anything could happen.

The progression of drug addiction is not pleasant to watch. It's also very odd how easy it is to see it in others but not in oneself. For many years, my focus was on Grant—I became consumed by his every move and diligent at lying for him to protect his supply for fear he really would kill me or hurt me a lot more than he was already doing. I didn't know how to look at myself or see my part. Our house became the meeting place for all our friends, and it seemed the only friends Grant had were also taking heroin or snorting cocaine and smoking joints. These activities became a normal part of everyday life. I loved seeing some of my brother's friends. They were almost three years older than I, and I always hoped that my brother would invite me into his room, but he never did.

When I was feeling confident, I would just march in and sit down and chat with his friends and my brother would let me stay for a while. But most of the time I would open the door a crack and my brother would yell, "Get out, you slut!" or "—you tart." If I was lucky I would get away without any physical damage. Emotionally, though, I was always bruised, yet I just kept repeating my behavior, knowing each time that I was putting myself at risk.*

---

* My parents seemed unaware that my brother was abusing me until he went into a drug-treatment program.

Treatment

By the time we were teenagers, my parents had bought a weekend flat, where they often spent long weekends, not knowing that Grant's disease had now taken full control. I remained silent as ever, thinking I could somehow fix everything. The parties started the moment my parents left and ran until the big clean-up moments before their return. All our friends would come over and the drugs would begin. My brother was a bully to everyone present, and more and more I felt ashamed of him and wished I wasn't connected to him in any way. Yet, when the friends had gone home and I found Grant in a drug-induced sleep in front of a blank, beeping TV screen, I would look at his pale face and dark eyes, knowing he really wasn't just a violent bully, he was as frightened and lost as I was.

I would sometimes drag him to bed or, at least, throw a blanket over him and pray that he would live till the next day. Once in my own bed, I'd try to sleep, but eventually I'd go back to his room just to make sure he was still breathing. Only then could I settle myself. I knew I ought to tell my parents and yet I was terrified. Grant had made me promise not to say anything. The truth was, I desperately wanted him to like me. I needed to feel connected to him. We both had a lot of healing to do, and although we didn't know it at the time, we couldn't help each other. But there was an unspoken understanding between us: we were both adopted and we could understand each other in a way our friends couldn't.

When I was nineteen, the manager of the restaurant where we both worked noticed Grant's problem. The manager took it upon himself to tell my parents. By then, Grant had been a heroin addict for three years. I remember my mother asking why I hadn't told her. I could barely answer. "I tried," I whispered.

My brother was sent immediately to a treatment center, and for a few years after treatment, he was involved in various recovery programs. While Grant was away, my mother decided to paint his room. She asked me to help her go through everything, because she felt that when he came out of treatment, it would be nice for him to come home to a fresh start.

As it was, the bedroom was painted an almost black color and the curtains were yellow from all the smoking. It was hard to believe that the rest of the house we lived in was so airy and clean. Just opening the door to his room was like walking into some squat in Kings Cross, where the buildings were run down and junkies lived with bare mattresses on the floor and records and rubbish scattered about. This room did not hold good memories for me. It was so strangely quiet without my brother lying on his bed watching television, an ashtray full of stubs balanced on his chest.

My mother got to work. When she does something, she does it fully and with much determination. I'd like to think I received that quality from her. We went through everything: each drawer, bookcase, cranny, and corner. Everywhere, we found the burned foil that my brother had used to "chase the dragon." (This is a method of ingestion in which the user places the substance on the foil, lights it from underneath, and inhales the fumes.)

My mother started painting and I watched her from the doorway, not helping at that moment and not really wanting to any longer. But as I watched her face, so intent on what she was doing and so wanting his room to look nice for him, I knew right then that she really did love us no matter what.

Why did that realization not make me feel any better? I thought love was supposed to make one feel whole. My parents loved us both very much, but they didn't understand how we felt. That was what frustrated me.

CHAPTER FOUR

Life with Drugs

When Grant left to go into treatment, it was the first time I had been alone. Life felt extremely dull without the drama, and it was then that my addiction began to take its toll. It was so easy for me to believe that, just because I wasn't using heroin, I didn't have a problem. I became very angry with both my parents and my brother. Suddenly, after everything he had put me through, he was getting all the attention. For a good few years, I kept my rage sizzling until it became too unbearable to live that way.

In retrospect, I see now that my brother was the catalyst for me to change and get the help I needed. In a strange way I am truly grateful, not for his terrible addiction, but that he cried out for help loud and clear. It got my attention and, ultimately, led me into support groups and into the work I needed to do to heal myself. I was able to stop focusing on him and to eventually demand the respect I finally realized I deserved. Grant knew it too, and changed his behavior toward me. Today, our relationship has improved dramatically.

But, at the time he went into treatment, I was still far from my own healing. Drugs seemed an incredibly easy solution to my problems. For one thing, they took away the wrenching pain in my heart and allowed me to function in the world without feeling constantly depressed and inadequate. Drugs also dissolved my separation anxiety. Suddenly I could stay away overnight whenever I wanted without any repercussions.

I smoked my first joint with my brother just before I turned fifteen. My girlfriend and I sat in his room and watched him smoke. That's when I decided to try it. My girlfriend was horrified but Grant was amused. He handed me a joint and they both stared as I told them I felt wobbly and strange. I giggled a little. But on the inside, I felt an awakening I had never experienced before. I felt alive! Perhaps life wasn't going to be so bad after all. Maybe, until that very moment, I just hadn't found the secret to happiness, and now, here it was! This was the connection I had been missing. This was the way to fill that terrible void.

Drugs were indeed a Godsend. My fears vanished. I could sleep. I felt invincible. I stopped caring what people thought about me. I had confidence. I began to wear sexy clothes and stopped hiding my bottom with big sweaters (for fear it was too large) and men became interested in me. This was a volatile mix, since at the same time, I was still handling being a teenager with all the emotions that come with puberty and trying to find myself. The fact that I didn't know who I was or where I came from just exacerbated my difficulties.

What was wrong with me? After all, I had a family, didn't I? Wasn't I grateful for that? I was so confused and mixed up, angry and afraid that the only solution was to make a strong commitment not to feel any of it. So, I blundered on with no sense of direction. I never gave any thought about what I wanted to do or achieve, and failed miserably at school. I could never concentrate or absorb any information that was given to me. If anyone had asked me what year I was studying in history, I couldn't have said. I had a lot of anxiety about failing and spent a great deal of time worrying.

The same year I smoked my first joint, I also started smoking cigarettes and, along with my girlfriend, to snort solvents in the form of typing correction fluid, which made us walk into walls and laugh hysterically. It took a while for the teachers to realize what was going on. They finally caught us after a girl, whom we had been threatening if she didn't give us her solvent, told the headmistress.

We were summoned to her office. My girlfriend and I stood before her huge brown wooden desk, piled with mountains of paper work that almost hid her from view. She was very short and very round and she always wore a black cape, like a cartoon superheroine. I thought she was in danger of being caught in a strong wind and lifted off her tiny pudgy feet.

We stood sheepishly side by side and waited for her to speak. Suddenly, I found her extremely funny looking. Since I was still slightly high from all that solvent sniffing, I started to giggle. My friend, who really couldn't stand straight from the effects of the stimulant, wobbled beside me and began to laugh, too. The headmistress seemed a little unsure of what to do, and I was certain she was trying to suppress a smile. Finally, she spoke in a loud, commanding voice. If we had any brain cells to begin with, she told us, we would surely lose them if we continued our current behavior. If we did not cease immediately, a letter would go to our parents. We managed a feeble apology and left the room still giggling. We went off to find a place to hide where we could have a cigarette and tell the other girls what had happened.

To the Precipice

College didn't change my behavior: I smoked dope, snorted substances, and spent my time arranging weekends and finding new men to fall in love with. I ended up taking a course in child development, as my mother felt it was important for me to have something to "fall back on." I was too scared not to follow her advice.

Addiction, I have come to learn, can take many forms. Before I went to any recovery programs, I truly believed that to be an alcoholic or a drug addict you needed to lose everything you owned and be sleeping under Waterloo Bridge. In fact, it is how those substances make you feel when you are using them and why you choose to do it that determine whether or not you are an addict, and the good news is that you don't have to reach bottom before you decide to stop. In my own case, using drugs, sex, food, and cigarettes only created more fear and more pain. Finally, they had such an extreme debilitating effect on me that I couldn't get on with my life with them or without them.

And then of course, there was the opposite sex, which gave me even more reason to feel depressed and take drugs. From the very beginning of dating, I could never be in a committed relationship. I began a pattern of going for men who were either so available they scared me, or completely unavailable in one way or another. That made it easy for me to see them as the problem and not myself. But often when the relationship was over, I would feel devastated. The feelings of separation were so powerful that I often wondered, "Why is this so intense? I really wasn't that interested, and now I feel like I can't be away from him."

I could write endless stories of all the drugs I took, the parties I went to, the blackouts, and all the so-called relationships, but I would rather tell you about what was underneath all that. No matter how many drugs I did or how many boyfriends I had, the moments of freedom from depression and fear were fleeting and, as time went on, the drugs barely covered my feelings at all. I so wanted to be accepted by people and had a terrible fear of rejection, yet I set myself up over and over by befriending people who would reject me or make fun of me, and boyfriends who already had girlfriends or wives. Ultimately there was never any real union or commitment. I was so sensitive to what people thought of me, and I couldn't bear for anyone to be angry with me. I always had to make things right. If my mother was mad at me, it was hard to get through a day at school. I would lose focus and concentration, and trying to hide that from my friends was very difficult. Smoking cigarettes and then sniffing solvents helped. I acted tough, was outspoken, and behaved wildly, traits for which I became infamous. The other girls laughed and I got attention, yet I never revealed to anyone how bad I felt inside.

I spent so much time living in my head, thinking, trying to figure everything out. I tried to control everything—how to get the drugs, how to get the man, how to make my friends continue to like me. At the end of a day, I'd be so exhausted that my inner fear often escalated to sheer panic. Trying to hide it all from others became harder and harder, and I didn't know how to tell anybody the truth.

As soon as college was over, I took a job as a waitress, which enabled me to maintain a lifestyle with no structure. Drugs and alcohol were forever available, and I became submerged in the night life, off to clubs after work to keep the party going and falling into bed at some early morning hour.

It was the eighties. Madonna was hitting the charts and I admired her attitude. I once heard her being interviewed. She stated that as a young child she had lost her mother, and I became riveted to the TV set as she talked openly about her loss. As I listened to Madonna, I felt a stirring inside and empathy for her. I never mentioned it to my friends. After all, they didn't see me as a child who had lost her mother.

I began to dress a little punky, wanting the lacy tights that seemed to be everywhere since Madonna had arrived, but they were so expensive. I went to the hip girls' shop and put on a pair in the changing rooms. Then I pulled my black leggings over the top, leaving space to reveal the lace from my calf down to the tops of my punky, pointy boots just like I had seen Madonna do.

"I must have them," I thought. I looked so cool! The need was incredibly strong, but the tights were so expensive. I didn't have that kind of money, and thought, "So poorly made," as I rolled down my leggings to cover them and walked out of the shop. I was thrilled as I realized I was going to get away with it.

Stealing became a justified way of life.

When I was twenty, and after my brother had completed drug treatment, I decided to join a band. It was something to do and my boyfriend at the time was very encouraging. He was part of the band, too, and we could be backing vocalists together.

He brought over a tape machine and recorded my voice over a song, pretending I had done the original backing vocals so it would appear as though I had some experience. In reality, all I had ever done was dance and sing in front of the mirror or with my girlfriends in their bedrooms, while we drank and smoked lots of dope.

I went for the audition and got the job. It was easy to see why; the lead singer took a fancy to me. It was fun, and something I had loved ever since my childhood days of writing out lyrics and singing every part. I loved music and the emotional release it provided. Unfortunately, after I joined the band, other things got in the way of the pure love of music. It all got a bit messy. I left the backing vocalist and took up with the lead singer. My former boyfriend was extremely upset and quit the band. A girl soon joined to replace him and we became good friends. It turned out that this new backing vocalist was working with established musicians. I was in awe of her: she was incredible and beautiful and she took me under her wing. She seemed to think I needed mothering! I was growing tired of waitressing and, hearing her talk about her career, I realized I wanted to make more of my life.

About four months after I started with the band, I was sleeping at her house when a record company called to ask if she knew another girl for a video and TV shows. Yes, she said, there was just such a girl at her house right now. The record company man came straight over to make sure I didn't have three legs and a hairy face. He brought with him the contracts he wanted me to sign for TV shows in case they decided to give me the work. He told me that if they couldn't get hold of another established backing vocalist, he would recommend me to the band in question. I would know the answer the next day. I couldn't quite believe what was happening and I tried to suppress my excitement for fear that it wouldn't work out.

The next morning, my friend woke me with a cup of tea, singing, "Zar got the job. Zar got the job." I was ecstatic and couldn't believe my luck. I had done only one gig in my life and, now, I was about to appear with a highly established performer on one of the most popular TV shows in London. There were plans for other dates as well.

The next two years were extremely busy as I traveled with different bands. At first, we would be in different countries for a day or two then, eventually, we went out on tours that took us away for longer periods of time. It felt so great to just pack up and get away from my mundane life, to live in a nice hotel surrounded by people who gave you attention just because you were one of "the band," to have my hair and makeup done before I went on stage to help promote the band's latest single.

I was always excited to be offered work, yet also terrified. Many insecurities surfaced as I became surrounded by established people. I felt like a fake and that, at any moment, someone would figure out I didn't know what I was doing, and I would be laughed at and fired. It is true what they say about sex, drugs, and rock'n'roll. It was all readily available, and a great escape for an insecure adoptee addict who needed to numb out all those feelings.

I was pretty naive in many ways, even though I had recently been hanging out in squats in London's Kings Cross area with some friends who were heroin addicts. In particular, I had a boyfriend whom I adored and often stayed with in "the buildings." They were structurally unsafe and ready for demolition any day, but somehow it all felt quite romantic. I'd take the tube from my parents' lovely neighborhood to the notorious area where pimps and prostitutes lurked at night, and I'd walk the long streets to "his" house, high as a kite and unafraid as men slowed their cars and asked, "How much?" I would raise my fingers to them and strut off, happy because I was going to get my boyfriend fix. He made me feel okay about myself, even if it was for just one evening.

But my life had begun to take a new turn. The musicians I was now working with were making something of their lives, they were successful, and eventually I managed to get away from all the heroin addicts. I wanted more for myself, but my new milieu became just another avenue for me to keep running from my problems. Drugs and alcohol were even more available and worse, it was acceptable to have dinner with a drink, to perform with a drink—and possibly some other substances to keep you going. After all, it was tiring to be up partying all night.

I began to watch intently how people behaved. How did the other girls in the bands act? How did they walk, talk, dress? I tried to imitate them, adding more swing to my hips and more makeup to my face and, for a time, I felt great. All the attention was intoxicating, but it never took away the real loneliness, the yearning for real friendship and companionship.

As I traveled regularly around Europe, it was wonderful to see so many interesting and beautiful places. We had a lot of laughs and played a lot of jokes on one another, but I was never able to enjoy myself to the full extent. My heart was being broken by yet another unavailable man. It was incredibly painful—I couldn't say no to him. I knew I was humiliating myself in front of the other band members, yet it didn't matter. I wanted to be with him, even though it was a no-win situation. I'd settle for a little rather than nothing at all.

As the months progressed, I continued to love singing and performing, but was unable to relax. I became more and more paranoid about what others thought of me. I was miserable and scared, and the void in my soul was becoming so big that neither drugs nor the unavailable man could fill it. I was okay while surrounded by people and parties and performing, but every time I returned home from a trip, a yawning emptiness threatened to overwhelm me, an emptiness that grew bigger when I was alone in the quietness of my home. The stillness began to bring me to my knees. I simply couldn't deal with my overwhelming feelings anymore. I couldn't keep up with the band's lifestyle and the pressure to look good, to stay thin, to be continually beautiful and in control. I was completely devoid of self-esteem.

I felt so insane, so full of fear and rage, that I found even the simplest of tasks stressful. Of course, I had always had feelings of rage that would come out in all the wrong places. Afterward, I felt extreme guilt, shame, and self-hatred. I had no control and, at that time, I didn't know that the bigger the rage, the bigger the fear, or that my chronic sadness was the grief of abandonment.

Some days, driving in my usual risky way, I contemplated aiming my car into a wall. I'd speed up, dodging cars, slamming on my brakes, and sticking my finger out the window and swearing at whomever I thought was in my way. If I thought I was right (which was usually the case), I would get out of my car and approach the motorist, who would either swear back or roll up the window quickly for fear of what I might do. My anger grew so big that I didn't care what happened to me—I just knew I wanted relief from these feelings.

I have heard many people say it wasn't a big crisis in their lives that led to change, just one small thing that made them realize they had had enough. It was the same for me. I could deal with hanging out with drug users in a dangerous part of London when I was seventeen, with my brother being put in treatment when I was nineteen, with my mother undergoing heart surgery when I was twenty-one. What I couldn't manage was regular day-to-day life.

The end of my drug use wasn't all that dramatic. Physically, I wasn't suffering too much—just short of breath from all those cigarettes. I hadn't lost a home, a job, money, a husband, or children as many other people do. But one day, all the drugs, the parties, the lure of the spotlight, stopped working for me. None of those things would ever make me feel better about myself. I remember sitting with a therapist I had met a few years before when my brother was in treatment. I believed then that I really didn't have a problem, that it was my brother and my parents. They just didn't understand me, they needed to sort themselves out, and the sooner they did, the better it would be for me. This kind man seemed to take an interest in me and listened to me open up slowly about my feelings. He appeared non-judgmental and was available to me every week.

For three years, he spoke to me gently, saying very little as I disappeared for weeks on end, drinking and drugging. I always came back with new stories of boyfriends who were too old or too married. Until that evening at the end of August 1987, as I was once again telling stories of woe, not many changes had taken place. On this particular occasion, he looked at me directly and said, "Zara, you are twenty-two years old and you are killing yourself."

I felt like someone had kicked me in the solar plexus. I knew at that moment, without a shadow of a doubt that he was right, and the truth was I couldn't stop on my own. I stared back at him, unable to speak. I always find that moment strange, because this man had told me the same thing many times before. But until that night, I simply wasn't ready to hear him. I left his office trembling. I knew something needed to change—and quickly.

I walked along the wet dark street and past a late-night news agent. The pull to go inside took me over, but I didn't buy alcohol. Instead, I bought chocolate, a few packets of various favorites, and started to rip open the packet before I was even out of the shop. Inside my head, a voice told me, "Zara, its over. You've got to stop."

"I can't stop, but I don't want to die," I replied to myself.

I made it into my friend's apartment where I was renting a room. She wasn't at home, and I was glad. I found my stash of dope and rolled a joint, telling myself to stop, but my hands had a will of their own. Fear seized my soul. I knew my life wasn't working, I knew in that moment I was in such trouble that if I carried on in the same way, I wouldn't live to be an old lady.

I had been attending some twelve-step meetings that were suggested when my brother entered treatment, and I remembered what they said: "Get on your knees and ask for help." I had thought it silly and embarrassing at the time, but now what did

I have to lose? Desperation overcame fear of how I would look, and weeping, I got down on my knees and prayed to God—or whoever was out there—in a way I never had before. Afterward, I lay down on my bed and felt an incredible presence that filled me with strength, a calmness I had never experienced before, a feeling that all was going to be okay, that I was safe, that I was cared for. Even though my face was pressed against the sheets, the darkness of the room lightened. I turned my head 'til I was looking upward at my curtainless window. The light was white and bright, but I couldn't work out where it was coming from. It seemed to stream straight through the glass from the night sky onto my bed.

"You're stoned, Zara," I told myself, and without further thought, I fell asleep.

CHAPTER FIVE

Healing Begins

When I awoke the next morning, the desire for drugs and alcohol was gone. Instead, I was suffused with the strongest desire to change my life and a willingness to take whatever steps were necessary to effect that change. From that day to this, I have never touched drugs or alcohol again even when I have wanted to.

When I began my sobriety, many friends said I really didn't have a problem, yet many recognized that I did. The truth of the matter is that my body probably could have taken more, but my mind and soul couldn't. The depression and pain were so severe that killing myself had begun to look like a reasonable option. Regardless of anyone else's opinion, they weren't living inside my head. I had reached a point where I had to make a choice: Did I want to live? Or did I want to die?

The change after that night when I had finally had enough was indeed miraculous. I began to attend twelve-step programs and held on to them like a shipwrecked woman to a life raft. Now, though, came the scary part: to walk into a roomful of people and listen to their stories was one thing, but to open my mouth and reveal what was inside me was terrifying. Nevertheless, once I did, I felt tremendous relief. And more, it also pushed me to look my demons squarely in the eye, to start taking responsibility for myself, and to not give up on this new chance at life.

I experienced such a wonderful high at the beginning of my sobriety—one having nothing to do with chemicals. I had an inner certainty that, at last, I was doing the right thing. That, finally, I could find relief from all the depression and pain. I truly could live another way, and I was thrilled. I remember zipping around in my little blue mini car, and shouting at the top of my voice my gratitude to God. I would meet up with all my new friends and they would laugh with delight. I was truly buzzing with a feeling that, no matter what anyone said, I had something I had never before experienced—peace of mind—and I was going to hang onto it tightly.

After a few weeks of sobriety, I was invited out bowling on a Saturday night by a group of fellow recoverees. I was horrified. *"Bowling!"* I exclaimed. "You go *bowling* on a Saturday night?!" I felt terribly depressed. Was this what my life had come to? What about all the parties and the gigs? Nevertheless, I decided to go. My new friends laughed at me kindly as I complained that my life was finally over. But I was so drawn to them. They had laughter in their eyes and a brightness I had never seen before. They were actually enjoying their lives, able to appreciate the simple things, and they weren't drinking or taking drugs.

So off we went to the bowling alley and—surprise!—I *loved* it. I got the knack of it quickly and suddenly became extremely competitive. It was fun and it felt real. I talked with strangers about life and feelings in a way I never had before, although at first, I wasn't ready to reveal too much. So mainly I listened and, as time passed, began to slowly let them see some of my tears. Showing my vulnerability was the hardest part and still is. Yet, paradoxically, it is the sharing of that vulnerability that leads to greater strength and acceptance; it is always healing.

The First Rejection

As I began my recovery around these issues, I slowly began to see that I had been repeatedly reliving that first rejection, playing it out in different ways instead of grieving the original loss. Adoptees are rarely told, "You need to grieve, because it is like a death to not know your mother. You can never replace her with a new one." But society is only barely beginning to recognize this and, for most of us, the grieving has to be done alone and hidden from others. I had carried that grief since birth, and only now did I begin to get glimpses of what was underneath my anger. I wasn't such a tough nut after all. I was scared and directionless and sad, and began to see that, yes, I did have feelings about being adopted. The jokes I had always made about myself, saying I was a mistake because I was probably the result of a one-night stand, were a cover-up for the fear that my mother had been raped, that I was the product of an act of violence.

My family knew I was attending meetings. It had been suggested when my brother went into treatment that we all seek some group counseling, but my parents didn't feel it was for them. Now, they would just ask me if I were going to a meeting. It wasn't a secret, yet like adoption, it was never discussed.

The Work Ahead

It became clear very early in my sobriety that a lot of changes had to be made. I wasn't going to get well overnight—that much was apparent. If I had known when I walked into my first meeting how much stuff I had to look at and how long it would take, I would probably have run screaming straight out the door again. I am glad I didn't know.

Those first five years showed me how much work needed to be done. Unfortunately, not all my friends could be happy for me, and I knew that staying sober depended on letting go of my old life. This was a terrifying realization: if I gave up those friends, that lifestyle, who would I be? For the first year, I carried on my same pattern of dating unavailable men. But now it was much harder because I had nothing to numb out those awful feelings. I tried desperately to pretend I could handle them, but it didn't work. Once again, I fell into a deep depression, and drugs began to look appealing. This time, though, I knew they would kill me and just didn't want to go down that road.

I had to give it all up—the boyfriends, the deceit—and live

on my own. I had to accept that maybe some women could sleep with married men or date men who weren't interested in a committed relationship, but I, Zara, could not. I *always* got emotionally involved, and it felt terrifying. But by now it was obvious that no one could make me whole, no one could fix me but *me*.

I was angry as hell. What, no relationships? No men to tell me I was okay, to lust after me? How could I cope without those affirmations? Who would I be? My identity came from the clothes I wore, the bands I was in, the men who pursued me. "It is too hard to do this!" I yelled at God. But I also knew it was too hard to live the way I was, stuck, trapped, dependent on outside sources for any sense of self-worth. A tiny voice within me said, "You have to try. It will be worth the effort."

New Image

When I was about a year sober, I realized it was time to start dressing differently. I had always dressed in a way that revealed body parts and got me the attention I craved, but now I knew that would have to change. Who would I be without this mask? I decided to do an experiment.

I packed up all my clothes—the red velvet backless number, the leather mini skirt, the skin-tight red dress with all those hooks up the back. Come to think of it, there were a lot of red things and a lot of black things! They had to go. After all, if the new me was about to reveal herself, she couldn't be wearing old-me clothes.

I vividly remember saying to myself a few years earlier as I stood in my fishnets, black velvet miniskirt, my favorite backless number, and wearing bright red lipstick, with a long cigarette dangling out of my mouth, "I just want men to like me for *me*!" Well, if they could have seen past the face paint, they might have. But in reality, all the paraphernalia of so-called fashion was a shield to keep everyone away. Genuine intimacy never entered my life.

Finally, all the clothes were tied up in bags in my flat. They had been there for a few days, when my friend Carol came to visit. I announced that I'd decided to sneak a few items back "just in case." "Just in case *what*?" Carol exclaimed. I was caught. I knew I had to be willing to change, to take the risk of not hiding anymore. I began to see how much I needed those clothes and that was pretty scary. After all, they were only clothes!

I began to choose a different wardrobe—less revealing and more conservative, yet still smart and stylish. These were things I had never looked at in the past for fear they weren't eye-catching enough. But as I began to find balance, I started to feel quite comfortable.

I also stopped wearing makeup. One evening I arrived at my parents house for dinner with relatives, and my mother, not knowing what was going on, asked me if I wanted to borrow her makeup, as she could see I wasn't ready!

Actually, once I stopped looking out the corner of my eye to see if the workmen would still whistle at me if I wore baggy clothes, I started to let go. The focus of my life began to change, it mattered less what people thought. It was as though I had stepped off the merry-go-round, and it was extremely liberating. I could now observe and realize that for me, the fast life didn't work; it brought only anxiety and despair. I began to experience a freedom I had never known before and a high on life that no drug had ever induced.

I carried on singing and performing, but this time as a lead singer in bands with people also in recovery or people who were moving in the same direction as I was. I began to write and write—songs of either hope and white light or the pain and anguish of reunion. Although some of these songs were not my best work, they helped channel the emotions without resorting to my usual escape of drugs, cigarettes, and a new man. I earned money by cleaning or baby-sitting. I was always broke, yet I was happier than when the money was easy.

I irritated many people talking about my new lifestyle. After all, it really wasn't for everyone, and I had, as usual, gone to the extreme. I still lacked balance and didn't know how to do anything in moderation. Many people stayed away as I preached and pranced in my new baggy clothes, celebrating a celibate life. But I felt so much hope, and knew I was more than just my clothes, and that relationships didn't have to be all bad and painful. I began to work harder on my relationships with girlfriends, and some wonderful friendships developed. Life began to roll along and I started to feel somewhat cured of the old me. I could function without drugs, and could live without a relationship. In fact, I became pretty independent and pretty overconfident—until one day across a crowded room I saw an extremely handsome man. Thus began my rapid descent from my high pedestal.

Since getting sober, I had gotten briefly involved with one man. Fortunately, I was able to see that a relationship with him would bring only pain, and managed to extricate myself. But for some reason, I couldn't see the danger with this new man. Maybe I felt a desperation that I really would end up alone, perhaps I forgot to trust myself. Nevertheless, it was a painful lesson. He did not want to marry me, he did not want commitment, yet why couldn't I leave? All this recovery and here I was again!

All the abandonment feelings came crashing back, except this time they were even more intense. Poor bloke, he understood there was something deep going on with me, but how could he really know? He decided to leave London and go back home to New York. The weeks before his departure were one of the most painful times of my life. I suffered terrible anxiety, and crying episodes were frequent. I began to feel absolutely insane, yet I couldn't walk away—I was staying to the bitter end. I also felt deep shame that anyone should see me so out of control. Even then, it began to dawn on me that the intensity of my grief didn't quite match the situation.

Yet after he had gone, I had a very difficult time. Deep loneliness and grief were, it seemed, continually with me. Some mornings, I would awaken in a panic, wondering how I was going to make it through the day, and I'd call friends to calm me down. One night, as I lay down to go to sleep, I found myself crying from a deep place. I cried about every relationship I had ever been in. I cried because I had never taken care of myself, and began to feel sorry for what I had done to *me*—I had treated myself so badly!

That night proved to be another turning point. When I awoke the next day, I made a pact with myself: I would never hurt myself in that way again. I would be a friend to myself, and if I couldn't have a marriage based on a real union, I would rather be alone. Anything less just wasn't worth the pain. I called a girlfriend, Gina, sobbing, and said, "Well, it looks like I will never get married and have children if I stay on this path. After all, I don't seem very exciting."

I look back on that experience and realize that each time I got involved in those situations, I felt extreme pain at the thought of separation. At the time, I never understood that any separation triggered the initial loss of my birth mother.

CHAPTER SIX

The Search

I needed to know who my birth mother was. This fact surfaced quite early in my recovery. I confided this to a man who had been helping me a lot at that time.

Why don't you?" he simply asked.

"What do you mean, why don't I?" I said, shocked. "Because I am not allowed."

Surprised, he pointed out that I was an adult and that in England, the records were open. I just had to take it one step at a time.

It appeared that all I had needed was a green light—someone to tell me it was okay. I threw myself into the search. It generated so

I am glad that I searched, since there was some serious medical history. I am resentful that the sealed record system prevented me from getting to know my birth mother.
—Dinah

much anxiety, though, that the only way I could get through it was to tell myself, "Zara, you don't have to meet her. Just gather the information." At that time, I earned an irregular living that gave me time to pursue the search. I worked as an extra on TV shows, did TV work with bands, and a little touring. But I had to be very careful who I was around, since my sobriety was so new and fragile. That led me to turn down some very attractive offers with bands. I also did babysitting, cleaning, auditioning, and singing in a band with other recovery people. Sometimes I claimed unemployment. Most of the time I was pretty broke, but

I had so much heavy emotional work to do that not being too busy was to my benefit.

Too afraid they would be angry, hurt, and would reject me, I never told my adoptive parents what I was doing. I needed the time to do my research alone and absorb each piece. I sent off for my information and was told I needed to see a social worker, who would assess my mental stability. Of course, they didn't quite say that, but I read the subtext. When I went to my first meeting with the assigned social worker I wanted to do my best to come across as a very well-adjusted human being. I didn't want to give anyone an excuse to keep things from me.

At the time, I was living in a bedsit. It was very small and my bed took up most of the room. Somehow, there was a fridge, sink, and even a shower squeezed inside, and with all my belongings, there was no room for anyone or anything else. Nevertheless, I was relatively happy living there. I needed a place to be alone, especially during "the search," where I could sit and cry if the need be or just stare at the wall, which I often did, when absorbing piece after piece of who I was.

The social services building happened to be just up the street from where I lived. I didn't know then that I had been born only a few streets away. Although I could easily have walked, on the day of my appointment I drove my little blue mini—anxious to get there as fast as I could. It was cold, mid-January, and the sky was almost as gray as the building. Approaching the steps to the main door, I could barely breathe, so I kept focusing on the door. I was almost floating; nothing felt real. I definitely wasn't in my body at all. I saw myself walking in and talking and yet I wasn't connected.

I had lived my whole life in an adoption fantasy story. I had been able to use it to keep people away from me, to not integrate. Up to a point, I liked the feeling of being different, that I had no ties to anyone, didn't belong to anyone. Now, I was going to find out that I was just like everyone else—that I, too, had a mother and a father (whoever they were), and that I wasn't just plunked here on earth by an alien starship. I had a birth story, too.

I cannot begin to tell you how strange it felt to notice how normal everyone seemed and how I felt no sense of connection. It was strangely quiet in the main hall. I walked to the receptionist and came face to face with an old school friend. We had traveled to Israel together, where we had drunk and partied and been thrown off the kibbutz where we were staying. Afterward, we had hitchhiked around Europe and ended up on a Greek island after selling our Walkmans for the boat ticket. One evening, thinking we had been given speed to help us dance all night long, we wondered why we were suddenly so sleepy that we began to pass out at the bar table with our Greek friends. When we showed them the package the tablets had come in, they laughed hysterically and told us we had been given sleeping tablets. I wandered back to our campsite, crawled into my sleeping bag, and slept for fifteen hours.

Sarah and I both smiled. I hadn't seen her in a few years since we had moved out of the flat we shared.

"I can't believe it!" she exclaimed. "I knew it had to be you—there could be only one Zara Samuels. I asked the social worker to tell me why you were here, but she wouldn't. You know, confidentiality and all that. Wow, it's so good to see you!" She looked at me expectantly.

"I am here to find out about my birth mother," I said, my mood still quite subdued.

"I had a feeling you were," she replied. Just then, the social worker appeared to show me into her office.

"Good luck," Sarah called. "Let us know what happens."

The social worker, Alice Clarkson, was a friendly middle-aged woman, strong in stature, with black hair, which I thought must be dyed. She was very chatty and quite excited by the prospect of helping an adoptee. She had never witnessed an adoptee following through with locating her birth parents. I was glad she couldn't see what was going on inside me.

We sat in her small, white-walled office with a large window overlooking the car park out front. She began to talk about my need for some help and counseling. What I was about to embark on could be very emotional, and it was always beneficial to talk about my feelings and expectations.

Immediately, I began to tell her about my wonderful recovery and that I had a special person helping me. The fact that this man knew little, if anything at all, about adoption didn't bother me at the time and she didn't ask. I convinced her that I had all the help I needed and had been working very hard on myself (well, only for a few months, but she didn't need to know that) and that I was ready for the information, thank you very much.

So, in her next breath, when I least expected it, she told me my birth mother's name. She had a file and she just said her name. It was that simple to her, but for me, it was the most incredible piece of information I had ever been given. I sat there, not knowing what to say. Stunned to think that it was that easy, that for all these years people had had access to my birth mother's name. It was too much for me to take in. I was a jumble of emotions, but the main thought running through my head was that my birth mother was real, she had a name, she existed. All the self-confidence with which I had walked through the door crumbled as I repeated over and over the name of this woman who was my mother.

We both decided that I had received enough information for one meeting, and I left as quickly as possible. Holding back my tears (God forbid the social worker should see the real me), I scheduled another appointment and somehow made it home.

The Great Detective

During the long wait between applying for my file and receiving it, I had a lot of time on my hands, so I found other things to do to keep the search moving. I went to Catherine House, where I had been so many years before with my schoolmate Nikki. There you can look at anybody's birth, death, and marriage certificates. It is an amazing place, a large building with miles of shelves crammed with files, and row upon row of tables where you can spread the files out to look down endless columns of names and dates. I enjoyed being there. The sense of anonymity was so nice; no one knew what I was doing, and no one bothered me while doing it. To think I had all these relatives who were just busy with their lives, and here I was tracking them down. I felt like this great detective who was uncovering the secret of life. Well, I was. It was the secret of *my* life.

The amazing thing about the place was that I could order anyone's certificates, and no one asked questions. When I found my birth mother's birth listed, I ordered the full version of her birth certificate. This would tell me the place of birth, the address where she had lived at the time, her parents' names and their occupations. I was told it would take three days and they could send it to me or I could come back and collect it. I chose to come back; it felt safer. Those three days felt like three years. While I queued up to collect the certificate, I remember expecting someone to demand to know what I was doing. When I finally got to the counter, they handed it over without interrogation and there it was—all the information, the address where she lived, the names of her parents.

At my next appointment with Alice Clarkson, I learned that I had been born in Finchley at a mother-and-baby home right around the corner from where I currently lived. My name was Paula Sampson. I was so shocked I wanted to cry. It never occurred to me that my birth mother would have named me. I had always thought of myself as merely a number. The fact that she had named me meant she had cared enough to think of a name, and I wondered why she had chosen Paula.

In a peculiar coincidence, when my adoptive mother worked with my father in his office, she called herself Mrs. Sampson, because she didn't want the clients to know they were related. As a child I asked my mother why she chose that name.

59

She explained that Sampson was easy to remember, since it was similar to Samuels. As a child, you accept what you are told, but when I found out that Sampson was my birth mother's name, I felt sick to my stomach. My mother tells me it is a coincidence.

Answers and More Questions

Now I could finally order my real birth certificate. Adoptees' certificates are different: all that is listed is your adopted name, date of birth, and names of adoptive parents. When I applied for my immigration papers in America, I was told that this birth certificate wasn't a valid document and I had to show them my first, original birth certificate. I have no idea what people do if they don't have that information. It is distressing to be told that your birth certificate is meaningless.

I went straight away to the neighborhood records office to order my birth certificate, which again was local to where I was living. I was terrified. But luckily, I hadn't yet given up cigarettes, and they helped numb my feelings as I chained-smoked my way through the ordeal. A chirpy little woman gave me the necessary paperwork and told me to fill it out; processing would take about fifteen minutes. As she busied herself with her work, I waited for her to ask me questions: What was I doing? Did I think it was right to request this information after all the hard work my adoptive parents had done? How it would break their hearts! How selfish of us adoptees to want to know who our natural parents were! Nevertheless, she didn't say a word except when I handed her the filled-out forms. "Thank you, Miss Sampson," she said. "Take a seat."

I nearly died. No, I wasn't Miss Sampson. I was Miss Samuels. I wanted desperately to explain, but couldn't speak. I sat down on a hard wooden chair and smoked some more. My head spun. Would my father's name be there? Would I get to know about him, too? What would it tell me?

Finally I was called. "Miss Sampson. Miss Sampson?" I think she said it only twice but I can't be sure. I was still getting used to the new name. I took the paper all folded up and went outside to the street, took a deep breath, and opened the certificate. I scanned everything quickly and then went back over it again slowly. There I was, Paula Sampson. That was me. Then it gave my birth mother's name, but where it said "Father," all I got was .... And the same with "Father's Occupation." Blank. I felt a pain in my heart, fleeting but sharp, and I numbed out. The one thing the certificate did give me was the address of where my birth mother had lived at the time of my birth. Maybe her parents were still there.

Getting Closer

I think I drove to that address within a couple of days. Too terrified to go alone, a friend came with me. It was in west London, not too far away, just down one long motorway, a road I had driven endless times. Now I was to find the building in which my birth mother had lived and carried me.

That street has never been the same to me since that day. Fifteen years later, I still look down the street at that gray two-story building and remember distinctly how I felt the first time I saw it. Now I tell whoever is with me, "That is where my birth mother lived when she was first pregnant with me."

It was easy to find the tall block of flats with a park opposite. I had a strong sense of having been in the park before, and the building had an eerie quality. I knew for certain my birth mother had sat in that park or at least walked through it while she was pregnant. We parked and I began to feel the fear set in. I had no idea if her parents still lived there, but I wanted to find out. It was easy to get inside. There was no intercom, or if there was, the door happened to be open, and there we were on the first floor, standing outside number two, the flat she had lived in, where she had found out she was pregnant, where they kept it a secret. I was trembling. What if someone opened the door? What if they *did* still live there? What was I doing and what in heaven's name was I going to say? There were some letters on the ground and I quickly picked them up to look at the name. It wasn't Sampson; someone else lived there now. I was flooded with two distinct emotions—relief and loss. Where were those people now?

I immediately said to my friend, "Let's get the hell out of here." Once outside, I stood for a brief moment and looked at the park again. Then we jumped in the car and drove off, giggling nervously.

Around this time, I finally received my adoption file. It arrived in a brown envelope that I still have. Alice Clarkson gave me some additional papers she wasn't supposed to and asked me to promise to never tell anyone; her job would be on the line. I went home and read over everything. It was the most painful, liberating, weird experience of my life. I was reading about a baby—Paula—me.

When I had my daughter, I started to wonder where I had been in my first three months of life and who had taken care of me. I had been adopted at three months and could see how attached I was to my daughter and how attached she was to me. I thought, how could my mother have done that?
—Doreen

I read how the mother had met an Italian student at a night club. She was sixteen years old and he was twenty-one. They had known each other only a short while when she became pregnant; he offered marriage, but she refused. (I was later to find out that the marriage offer was not true.) The birth had been hard for my mother. I was with her only about a week when she became too sick to care for me. Twelve days later, I was placed in foster care. I have never found out where I was or whom I was with for those twelve days. Eventually, suitable parents were found. Materially they were able to provide a good home. The woman was a fine homemaker and the man was a lawyer. They also had a little boy, adopted two-and-a-half years earlier. I thought, isn't it interesting that adoptive parents don't adopt just two boys or two girls? They can create the perfect family with the perfect age difference.

One of the most difficult things I learned was that my adoptive parents were interested in me, but that they had already booked their winter holiday for two weeks. Could they pay the fostering fees and pick me up when they got back? I didn't understand how they could not have dropped everything. Didn't they understand that two weeks to a baby without a regular mum was a lifetime? They finally came to meet me on January 4, 1965. They took me home for the usual probation period with a view to adopt. At the age of two months, I was with my third mother.

Intuition

After reading all the papers, I cried all night long. I was crying for my whole life. I felt grief from the deepest part of my soul. I also felt very strongly the rage I had always carried, but this time I knew why I was so angry. A bunch of strangers had planned my future without consulting me. Who the hell were they to know what was best for me and where I should be packed off to? I felt as though my birth mother just wanted to get rid of her little problem and get on with her life, while my parents wanted to pretend that I was really their child and that I had had no life before them. I didn't feel chosen or special—just betrayed.

I was deeply saddened to find out my birth mother hadn't been in love with my father, that it had been just a casual affair. Perhaps that was naive of me, but I was still young. Even though I would joke, "I was probably the result of a one night stand," I hadn't realized how much I had hoped for a different reality. The truth was devastating, and it also confirmed what I had always believed about myself—I was a mistake.

I spent the next few weeks going back and forth to Catherine House and deciding how to get more information. I remember one day looking through file after file for my birth grandmother's information and realizing the name didn't match what I had— it was a slightly different spelling. I stood for a while probably looking confused, when out of the crowd a man approached me and asked if he could help. I told him my situation and he said that he helped adoptees trace their families and was writing a book on the subject. He made some suggestions. I showed him the names that all seemed so similar yet were spelled differently, and he asked, "Which one do you feel is right?"

I read one out and said, "I am so sure it is this one. I feel there is just a spelling mistake." "Trust your intuition," he advised. "So much of a search is about that."

Well, I thought, *that's all very well for you to say, but don't you know who I am? I can't do that! How can I trust that part of myself? It has so often got me into trouble!* But the odd thing was, I did begin to trust that voice. It was so strong that I just knew which way to go, as though my whole being was pulling me. The name I chose proved to be the right one, and the stranger just seemed to disappear into the crowd.

By looking through every month of every year that I considered my birth mother was of marrying age, I found out that she had eventually gotten married. There were columns and columns of names, and hers would have been so easy to miss—the writing was so cramped and small. Finding that piece of information gave me a tremendous feeling of accomplishment and I actually became very impressed with myself. I seriously thought I would make a great detective one day, solving mystery after mystery, but I also realized I was jumping the gun. I had to solve my own mystery first.

I ordered the marriage certificate, which told me that she had married an Italian man who worked as a chef. They were living in Knightsbridge at the time. Although I knew he couldn't be my birth father, I couldn't help wondering why she had again chosen an Italian. Marrying outside the faith doesn't usually go down well in Jewish families, and I wondered how her parents had felt about that.

I continued to look through each year and discovered they had had a son. (A daughter had been born within a year of their wedding, but I didn't find this out until later). I ordered the son's birth certificate, but couldn't find any other children after him. He was only about twelve years old, and I thought, *Youngest child, most recent address.* The certificate told me where they had been living at the time of his birth. Once again, it was close to where I lived at the time. That was always the strangest part for me—how close to one another we had all been living. Had we passed one another in the car, sat next to each other on the same bus, shopped at the same stores? I had always wondered if we would instantly recognize one another, if I could have picked her out of a lineup.

Once I had this recent address, I dragged Kelly out with me again. When we arrived on the street in question, I hid, petrified, in the car and sent her off knocking on doors. Kelly's story was that my birth mother had been a school mate of her own mother, and that she wanted to invite her to a reunion. I had fantasies of people saying, "We are not fooled by your story! We know it's that bastard brat trying to ruin her mother's life. She was given up once—doesn't she get it?"

There were other scenarios, but they always had the same ending: REJECTED in big red letters.

I am not looking for a mommy. After all, I am fifty. [But] I feel that I have the same rights as everyone else: the right to know.
—Elinore

After a while, Kelly came back to tell me that there had been no answer at the actual address, but that she had knocked on a neighbor's door. The neighbor told her the family had moved a while back but that she didn't know where. She suggested Kelly call a certain person who lived down the street, because the two families had been ever so friendly; they would surely help her. I think she even gave Kelly the telephone number.

Wow, I thought, *some neighbor! The next thing you know she will be telling us all the dirt on number 47 and that Mrs. So-and-So at number 56 is definitely shagging the postman.* Kelly managed to get away before that happened, and I thanked God for all the gossipy, nosy people in the world. This anonymous former neighbor was a huge key in helping me find my birth mother.

I probably drove Kelly nuts over the next few weeks, but she is much too nice to say so. I would go over to her house and she would dial the number and I would shallow breathe, watching her every move. But there was never any answer, and I began to feel despondent. We decided that Kelly should try to call at different times during the day, and that I didn't need to be there every time, but that was hard to let go. Then I kept calling Kelly to ask if she had tried to phone that day. My poor friend didn't have time every day, so in the end we decided I should try on my own. What a concept! I had been too scared to speak on the phone in case the former neighbor recognized my voice, in case I sounded exactly like *her*. Talk about paranoia!

So I did call and, eventually, I had some luck. At last a young girl answered and I told her my made-up story. "Oh yes, I know them," she replied, then said a girl's name, whom I realized must be my sister, and then my brother's name. For a split second I couldn't speak. *Wow, I have a sister, and wow, she knows them! They exist, they are alive!* I managed to compose myself and tried my best to sound as though I was someone who merely needed some casual information. Then she told me they had moved out of London about a year earlier and my heart sank. Did she know where? No, she didn't, but she was sure her mother did. Her mother would be over at her house on Saturday night for a big party, and I should call to speak to her then.

My head spun in a million directions. What if they had moved to Italy? How would I ever find them then? In one way, it seemed I was so close, yet it also felt hopeless. I was scared of knowing and scared of not knowing. It was a very uncomfortable place.

I immediately went and ordered my sister's birth certificate. Her name was Roberta. My best friends in childhood, two sisters who lived across the street from me from when we were toddlers, were called Katie and Roberta. The three of us had been inseparable. I loved those sisters so much (I still do), and felt so close to them growing up. I thought of them as my closest friends and so desperately wanted to be their sister. But at night when I had to go home and leave them together I felt sadness. The truth was, I wasn't their sister. They had a special bond that real sisters have, and I knew that, as much as they included me, I could never be part of that unique connection. Now, twenty-four years later, I was to find out that I had a sister all along, and her name was Roberta, too.

The day finally came for me to call the neighbors' house. I was terribly nervous and said a quick prayer before dialing. I say "quick" because it was so hard to be still even for a moment. A girl answered the phone, her voice battling against the background of party sounds, people talking and music playing. It was the same girl who had answered before. I reminded her who I was and that she had said to call that night. Was her mother there, I inquired, and could I speak with her? She told me to hold on and I heard her shout, "Mum, there's a girl on the phone." I couldn't hear anymore, just the phone dropping down and the muffled sound of the continuing party. I felt sick. At last the girl came back to the phone and said very casually, "Me mum said they moved to Weybridge."

My heart leaped.

"Weybridge," I repeated, just to make sure.

"Yeah, she said they opened an Italian restaurant down there."

I stammered "Thank you," and we said goodbye.

She didn't ask me a million questions, she didn't wish me luck, she just gave me the information and was gone. Now if someone had called me wanting to know where someone I knew had moved too, believe me, I would have given them the third degree and tried to find out what the scandal was about before I revealed anything. (Well, some of us are sicker than others.)

So there I was with a crucial missing piece of information. I was tired and freaked out. It was as though I had always known

I would find out, yet I was aware that really knowing the truth meant crushing the fantasy I had lived in for so long. Until now, my birth mother could be anybody I wanted her to be, depending on my mood that day. Now I was going to find out the truth, and that could mean rejection. She might not want to know me at all. But I also knew if that were the truth, I would handle it somehow. I just had to keep moving forward.

CHAPTER SEVEN

Reunion

The next day, I went with a friend to visit her sister, who had had a baby a few months before. We really looked forward to the visit, and not only because of the new baby. The sister lived on a houseboat in west London. The canal was beautiful, so green and calm, and although the houseboat was a little rickety-looking from the outside, the inside was delightful. It was warm and cozy, and it was so much fun to sit in the lounge and look out the window onto the water. The baby, a little girl, was so appealing. She sat in one of those bouncers going up and down with such a funny expression on her face that soon we were all crying with laughter, which made her squeal and laugh, too.

I began to update my friends on my search. I told them that only the night before I had found out where my birth mother had moved to. The sisters looked at me and said almost in unison, "Weybridge is just over there, the next town from here," and they pointed across the water.

Geography never having been my strong point, I managed to mumble an "Oh," then an "Oh, God!" I looked out suspiciously over the water, as if my birth mother and family might suddenly appear before me.

My friends suggested I call directory inquires right away and get the phone number.

"Do you want business or residential?" the operator asked. She was just an ordinary woman going about her business of giving out a zillion numbers a day. She would never know the significance of what she was about to tell me.

"Both," I answered. I wrote down and double-checked the numbers, then hung up quickly. No bolts of lightning came out of the sky, no special music or loud booming voice announced to the world that ZARA SAMUELS HAS LOCATED HER BIRTH MOTHER.

I looked back at my friends, whose eyes had been riveted on me the whole time. "Did you get it?" they breathed excitedly. I nodded. "Dial it," one of them said.

For a moment I froze. "Okay," I said presently, "but be quiet. I am not going to say anything." With trembling fingers, I dialed the number. A woman answered whom today I know to have been my birth mother. I let her say "Hello" a couple of times and then I put the phone down.

I asked my friends for a local phone book and got the addresses of both their home and their restaurant. I am still amazed at the series of coincidences that led me that day: that I was at my friend's houseboat so close to Weybridge, that of course she would have a local phone book. It was all so easy, and during that time I felt carried, like there was some force steering and guiding me. When my old fear of rejection came up, I used all my experiences and so-called coincidences to remind myself that I was meant to complete this search and that no matter what, I would be okay.

Approaching Slowly

I wasn't ready to make contact immediately. I needed time to absorb all that I had found out, and of course I needed to spy. I dragged another girlfriend, Wendy, along since it felt too scary to go alone. I say, "dragged" my friend, but she was quite willing. My venture seemed to be exciting to other people, and they wanted to be involved. As for myself, I was mainly out of my body. It all felt so unreal and too painful to fully connect with what I was doing.

I made the journey to my birth mother's house a week later with my girlfriend helping with directions. As we turned down her street, I thought my heart would jump out of my mouth. It was a small suburban lane with little room between houses, although the houses were a nice size with expensive cars in the driveways. Her house was almost hidden behind bushes, and we found a good place to park on the opposite side of the street where we had some view of the windows and part of the driveway. I had the same feeling that I'd had on the previous search for her house—that I would be recognized immediately. I slid down in the seat for safety, drinking juice and eating the sandwiches I had made, which Wendy found highly amusing.

Sitting upright, she stared at the house. She was talking as I munched away, saying things like, "Oh, how sad, your mother is in that house. I sense she must be sad, too." I wanted to throw up. I just couldn't deal with those thoughts. As I was watching Wendy's reaction to it all, someone walked out of the house. The blood rushed to my head. It was a man, average height and build, with a moustache, in his early forties. He walked to the edge of the driveway and stood for a moment. He noticed our car and for a split second stared directly at us. At that moment, a group of boys cycled past, and one shouted, "Orlando!"

"That's your brother!" my friend cried. It was hard to tell which one he was as they were going quite fast, but my friend got really excited. She was convinced she had spotted him. The boys cycled off and the man went inside. We waited quite a while longer but saw no one else. As we drove away, I felt so relieved. I drove up again a couple more times before actually making contact. I also managed to find their restaurant. It was closed that day, but I looked through the window.

I felt happy that everything—the house, the restaurant—looked so normal. As an adoptee with no information, I had lived a great deal in fantasy about my true heritage. One moment, believing my birth mother was a famous movie star, and then the next, she was in prison for murdering her best friend. Or, that she was a hooker living in a squat in Kings Cross. To know that she lived in a normal-looking house with a normal-looking car brought me a huge sense of relief, although maybe I was slightly disappointed she wasn't royalty.

The Meeting

I wish I could tell you that reuniting with my birth family fixed everything in my life. It didn't. What it did do was to fill a lot of empty spaces in my heart. Just by knowing the facts, the real truth, I have been forced to give up the fantasy and look at it all squarely in the eye. This has brought up tremendous pain, deep feelings of abandonment and despair that I know now were always there, buried deep in my heart.

Nevertheless, reunion began the process of feeling all these emotions. It was like slogging through a swamp full of alligators and snakes and unseen predators. I am not sorry I found my birth family. It was something I needed to do for myself. I am sorry, though, that it was not all that I had hoped for. Only later did I realize that my expectations had not been realistic.

Not long after I found out where my birth mother lived, I called Alice Clarkson. We talked about the next stage, contacting her. Should we write? Should we call? We jumbled around ideas, but nothing felt good to me—there were so many *buts*. "But what if we send her a letter and her husband doesn't know and he opens it and he turns into a raving monster and leaves her?" I would say, or "What if she reads it at breakfast and chokes on her toast?" or "What if she really has no memory of even having a baby?" The list went on and on and the social worker tried to be reassuring. Personally, I don't think she had a clue either. She was more excited by the fact that in her whole career I was the first adoptee who wanted to complete the reunion with her help. Maybe the other adoptees had more self-esteem than I did at that point because I just wanted to be told what to do. Actually, I didn't know there was another option, that adoptees and birth families could reunite in any way they chose. I still felt that I wasn't really going to be allowed to do this.

The thought of actually calling made me feel sick, so a letter felt like the safest of all the options. It gave me a little more time to compose myself, and we wrote it in a way that gave my birth mother a chance to deny her past if her husband or family didn't know. I was still into protecting everyone, but it was the only way I could handle it. After several revisions—I felt that every word was important—I finally had the letter in hand.

Dear Mrs. Giocondi,

I am trying on behalf of my client to trace members of a family to whom she believes she may be connected. The name of the family she wishes to trace is Sampson, and they lived in the Eagling area around 1964.

If you feel you can help and would like to discuss this further, then contact me either by letter or by telephone at the above number.

In all cases where one is trying to trace members of families who have lost touch, it is common to write to people who, in fact, have no connection with the people involved, and if this is so, I am sorry to have troubled you.

Yours sincerely,

Mrs. Alice Clarkson*
Social Worker

I held onto the letter for a couple of days and went to my recovery groups and cried and cried. Although everyone was kind, no one really knew what to say. The truth was those groups were not about adoptees and no one had any answers for me. A wonderful thing did happen, though. I heard a young woman

---

* I have changed her name to protect her privacy.

share that she had recently met some family. Although she was quite vague, I just knew she was adopted. I grabbed her at the end of the meeting, and she said, yes, she had just been reunited with both her birthparents. They were married to one another, and she had three full-blood sisters. We talked a lot, and during the next few weeks she stayed in contact. We became close friends and still are. We continue to talk about the impact of adoption and how we can work the tools of recovery to help us heal. I am truly grateful she is in my life.

I knew I had to post the letter eventually, but I was so scared. Actually mailing it meant there would be no turning back, that I would really know the truth. The fear of rejection was so strong, but finally the not knowing became unbearable. I dropped the letter into a letter box. Immediately I was engulfed in a wave of panic and dashed off to meet with some friends. Once again, I cried and cried. "I want the letter back! What have I done?" I fantasized about running to the letter box and clinging to it until the postman came so that I could take it back. Yet I knew I had to face this stuff sooner or later, and the truth was I would never really feel like it.

For the next few days, I drifted in a limbo state. I was very jumpy, I couldn't focus on anything, and, looking back, I really don't know what I did to get through the wait. The days felt endless, and every time I went back to my bedsit, I would unlock the door with trepidation and go to the answer phone to see if there was any news. My adoptee friend often called to check in with me. It was a relief to talk to someone who understood.

Secrecy

During all this time, I never told my parents what I was doing. I wasn't ready, so it felt very strange when they called to see how I was, to say that all was okay, and to keep everything back. I was too scared that my mother would be hurt. I needed to focus on myself, and I could not risk taking on my mother's feelings, something I always did in those days. I was also a very immature twenty-four-year-old who was as terrified of my adoptive parents' rejection as I was of my birth mother's.

The strange thing about my search and being an adoptee was that I had never read a book on adoption. I read every other kind of self-help book, but it was so instilled in me that adoption shouldn't be an issue. Although my insides screamed out for some identification, I simply went along with the accepted wisdom.

Letters and Photos

About four days after I mailed the letter, I came home to a ringing telephone. I unlocked my door quickly and lunged for the phone. It was Alice Clarkson, and she talked very fast in an excited voice while I listened as hard as I could. "Yes, your mother is delighted! She really wants to meet you. She knew one day you would search. Her children have never been told so she needs some time to tell them. Her husband always knew . . . she would love to meet you straight away, but the problem is she has relatives coming to stay and then the whole family is going to Italy for three weeks. So it would be best we waited until they get back . . . Would you write her a letter and send her a photo?"

I was thrilled and amazed. I asked more questions, like, "What did she sound like?" and "Are you sure she was really happy to hear from me?"

I felt a bit disappointed that she wouldn't meet me for a while. It was strange that she, too, like my adoptive parents, had a holiday booked just as I showed up. Nevertheless, in this case I was relieved. Letter writing, for the moment, felt safe. I asked the social worker what to write and she advised me to keep it simple; I didn't need to tell my whole life story yet; there would be plenty of time for that.

I do remember sitting down to write the letter, staring at the blank page for a long time. I was writing to my birth mother and it didn't feel real. How should I word things? What do you say to a stranger who happens to be your mother? I kept the letter very brief, telling her what I was up to in my life, but I didn't go into detail about my emotional state. I thought it wise to save that stuff for later! I did spend a long time choosing a photo to enclose. After all, I wanted to look really good! I ended up sending one from a holiday when I was tanned and my hair had just been blow-dried. She didn't need to know I was back to my pale-faced self; she'd find that out soon enough.

I received a letter back from my birth mother soon after. As I held the envelope in my hand, I began to shake—more than anything else, I wanted to see her photo. I ripped the letter open.

When I look at my son, I see photos from my own childhood. We are so similar in looks and coloring that people mistake my baby photos for my son's. It's wonderful! It makes me realize how much I've missed being able to look at family members and see similarities and feel like I belong—like we belong to each other. I had always been envious of my husband's family and their strong resemblance to each other. Now that I have someone who looks like me, I wonder who else we look like. Is there an uncle we take after? Or a grandma? Or the obvious question: do we look like my birth mother or father?

—Fiona

Enclosed was a recent Polaroid of her. I think she, too, had just blow-dried her hair, and she was smiling in a nervous way. It struck me that whoever had taken the picture was joking with her about something, trying to get her to relax. I studied the photo for a long time. I looked at it in different lights, even taking it to my window to see her as clearly as possible. She wasn't what I had expected.

But what had I expected? A two-headed freak? A disfigured face? I didn't really know, but I could see the similarity between us straight away. She looked so young, so normal. There I was again, saying *normal* as if it was a strange thing. Whatever I expected, it wasn't *normal*. Looking back, I believe it was because I was seeing a reflection of myself for the first time, and I had no real concept of what I truly looked like. And deep inside me was the belief that my mother had given me away because I was ugly, that in some way I was disfigured.

I opened the letter and began to read.

Dear Zara,

Thank you for your letter and photograph.

You're a beautiful girl, but I knew you would be. You were such a beautiful baby.

I've always hoped that one day you would contact me, but now it's happened, I can't quite believe it. Since I spoke with the social worker I can't seem to stop crying.

I felt extremely nervous and apprehensive at the thought of meeting this stranger who happens to be my daughter, but on seeing your photograph, I can see that you are not a stranger but someone who is very familiar to me.

She described her family and then told me that she wouldn't be able to meet me for a while, as she was going on holiday for three weeks. Once again, I marveled that my introduction to both my mothers was delayed by their holidays.

We exchanged a few more letters before she went away, and I learned a little about my brother and sister. She also told me about how she met my birth father, that he was a student working in Soho as a waiter, and that they had met at a club called Les Enfants des Terribles, "the terrible children."

Dear Zara,

You can imagine my parent's shock. "Nice Jewish girls" just did not get pregnant. I was sent to a mother-and-babies home in Finchley, and after you were born I was meant to stay at the home until you were six weeks old. Unfortunately, the day after you came back, I became ill and was rushed back into the hospital. You were then placed with foster parents, and I only saw you once more when I had to take you to the court to sign adoption papers.

It's always been my deepest regret that I could not keep you, but I was a very immature seventeen-year-old, and without the support of my parents I would never have managed.

I adore my children but there's always been something missing in my life. No child can replace another.

Love,
Pat

Some of the words were comforting: that she had wanted to keep me meant so much, yet it was still truly hard for me to understand why she hadn't. I could not at that time put myself in her shoes.

I longed for more detail about my birth father, but it all seemed rather vague and I was too scared to ask for more. I was very guarded and unsure of how to be.

Birth Father

I know this sounds crazy, but I had never really thought about my birth father before I met my birth mother. Now I don't want you to think I had ideas that I was the product of immaculate conception (well, maybe it did cross my mind). I just never thought about him. As a child, all I focused on was my mother. It was only when I received my birth records at age twenty-four that I began to realize, "Oh yes, there had to be a man involved in this somewhere." I had always felt like I was planted on the earth somehow, that I didn't arrive like other people did.

I must say that finding out he was Italian felt great to me. I always had a thing for Italy and thought the women quite stylish. Well, let's face it—Italy has gorgeous clothes. Upon finding out I was Italian, I immediately remembered an incident from a few years earlier with my adoptive mother. I had always liked crosses, though never thought of them in a religious sense. They were spiritual symbols to me. I had a huge wooden cross hanging in my bathroom and a smaller cross with rosary beads that I had bought at the Vatican. All the time, unaware I was half Italian.

My mother popped over to my flat and went to use the bathroom. The next thing I heard was a big howl. "How could you!" she shrieked.

It took me a moment to realize that it was the cross that she was mad about, and I reassured her that it meant nothing as far as religion went; I just liked it. She was very upset and believed it was a great insult to Judaism. I had not meant to offend anyone; I just felt very drawn toward it, and kept saying, "It's from Italy, the Vatican in Italy. It is just a reminder of the power Italy had for me."

My Italian Side

My girlfriend Melanie came over to take me out a few nights later. As I came out of the front door, she said, "My, aren't we looking Italian today!"

We laughed a lot, but it felt so good, so freeing. The funny thing was that we had worked together as backing singers and we had toured Italy. The whole time we were there I kept complaining about how crazy the people were and that I didn't understand why they had to shout so much. And all the time I was one of them.

Melanie flew me to Italy later on that year as a birthday present. She was working there and she wanted us to be together again in Italy, this time with me knowing who I was. It was a very different experience. I looked at everyone on the street, at their features, their coloring, and I could see the similarities. An old man started chatting with us—well, flirting, actually—in a market, and he asked us where we were from. We said London and then I happily told him I was half-Italian, which made him laugh and pinch my cheeks. I laughed, too. All the questions I had carried for so long and the emptiness of not knowing had slowly begun to fill up.

Face-to-Face

I met my birth mother at the end of the summer of 1988. She telephoned the social worker and we set up a meeting at Alice's office, which was walking distance from my flat. The night before, I went into complete panic and obsessed about what to wear. There it was again—my old friend Appearance Obsession. It gave me a false sense of control, and of course I had to look acceptable so I wouldn't be rejected. I believed that looking good would help cover up all the turmoil inside.

On the day of the meeting, I walked slowly up the street noticing my every breath, my every step. I wanted to be very dramatic and thought about all the movies I had seen where long-lost relatives see each other for the first time. I imagined a camera crew filming me and wondered if I was reacting in the right way. After all, I was about to meet my birthmother and was sure that one took on a certain look for that role.

I looked at everyone else on the street that I passed, just people going about their business, running for a bus, or grabbing a newspaper. I wanted to stop them and say, "Hey, do you notice how different I look today? I am going to meet Her, the woman who gave birth to me, the woman I have imagined since the day I was told as a young child that I had been given up for reasons that still don't really make sense to me."

Nobody seemed to notice me as I walked more and more slowly up the street. When I finally arrived at the office, all the bravado that had carried me there crumpled. I wasn't in a movie. This was real. I began to have a panic attack.

I vaguely remember Alice Clarkson taking my arm and leading me up the stairs. My mother, she said, was already there. My breathing got shallower and I muttered, "No, wait! I can't!" But she didn't listen and before I knew it, she had opened a door. I turned around and there were my birth mother and her husband.

They both stood up. The husband, with tears streaming down his face, hugged me and I began to cry. My birth mother, dry-eyed, hadn't moved. I walked over to her and kissed her, and we all sat down. Then they all began to talk at once. I just sat, unable to speak—I felt numb. I was glad for their chatter because it gave me time to glance at her, to study her. I thought how different she looked from what I had imagined my mother would look like. I couldn't tell at that time whether she was attractive or not. I saw a lot of similarities between us; it was different from looking at a photo. Her mannerisms were so much like mine: the way she dressed, the jewelry she wore, it was so much my taste. She looked very well put together and I could tell she took great pride in her clothes. I wondered if she had worried about what to wear as much as I had. Her shoes were very stylish, I thought, and her feet weren't particularly big, so I didn't get that from her. Mine had always been exceptionally large, which caused me great anguish. I saw that her body type was just like mine, too: she was slim and in good shape with olive skin much like mine. I was, however, a good few inches taller than she, which surprised me a little.

We sat for I don't know how long. I remember thinking how green the room was and how much it needed a good paint job. I sat alone on a big faded armchair that had lost its spring. I didn't want anyone near me at all. My birth mother sat to my right on a hard-backed chair that made her sit stiffly upright. She seemed so contained, so in control of her emotions, yet I sensed that a lot was brimming underneath.

Motherhood is the most healing thing. To have the intimacy and the connection and to look at her and see reflections of myself are profound. Her personality is like mine and I just know her.

—Gayle

I liked that I could sink back into my chair. Its big arms around me gave me a feeling of safety and a place to hide the tears that constantly streamed down my face. I felt ashamed of them, and wished that she, too, would cry so I wouldn't be alone with my feelings.

My mother's husband sat off to the left, not quite in the group, and I continued to watch as they talked to the social worker, who did her best to keep the conversation going. I was still unable to speak. Nothing felt real. If I could just watch like an observer I would make it through. "I will think about it all later," I told myself, hoping to distance myself and stop my tears. I didn't want to linger too long on any feelings. I felt so vulnerable and wished I had someone with me.

The social worker, thinking she had to be a social worker, kept asking us questions, like "How do you feel?" and "Isn't this incredible?" I felt mainly numb. After a while, we decided to go and have some lunch.

We went to a local restaurant. Despite the gravity of the situation, my primary emotion was guilt. What if someone I knew came into the restaurant, or worse, a friend of my family? Even though I knew in my head that that I had every right to know my heritage, in my gut there always lurked a feeling of betrayal toward my adoptive parents. I have had to work very hard to banish those voices.

Once inside the restaurant I felt a little more relaxed and the tears stopped. I began to listen eagerly as my birth mother told me about the family. She talked a lot, which was exactly what I wanted. I needed to know as many details as possible. She told me that she had revealed me to my brother and sister and that both had reacted differently. My sister Roberta was excited but upset that she hadn't been told before; my brother, Orlando, on the other hand, took one look at his mother's serious face and thought she had killed his cat. He was so relieved to know the cat was all right that all he said when she told him about me was, "Oh, okay," and carried on with what he had been doing. Everyone thought this was extremely amusing, but I wasn't quite sure what to make of it.

Over lunch, we made arrangements for me to visit their house to meet Orlando and Roberta. They gave me directions, not knowing that I had already been there. After an hour or so, we finally parted. I was relieved to get back to my place and to be alone.

I would just love to look my birth mother in the face, but my adoptive mother would be crushed. She's all alone in this world other than our family. I have not begun my search so as not to crush her.

—Helen

CHAPTER EIGHT

Moments of Reunion

I will not bore you with all the times I have met with my birth family because over the last fifteen years there have been many. I will highlight only the most impactful—those days that left me just barely making it out of their house, waving happily goodbye and then howling uncontrollably all the way home. They have seen me cry, but the howling I prefer to do in private.

I met Orlando and Roberta about a week after my first introduction to my birth mother and her husband. It felt strange to drive to their house knowing that this time I would be going in. I was nervous and excited at the thought of meeting my siblings. I parked outside, took a long, deep breath, and knocked on the door. Pat and my sister opened it together. Roberta and I looked at each other, smiled and said, "Hello." I felt instant connection and fondness, pure and uncomplicated. We were both awkward, and giggling seemed to ease the moment.

Until I met my brother, I had never seen anyone else who looked like me.

—Irene

Roberta looked like me: round cheeks, similar eyes and eyebrows, which I noticed straight away. I was good at analyzing faces—I had done it for years. Picking out the similarities in the faces of biological relatives faces had almost become a pastime.

I longed for Roberta and me to be alone together, to find out who she was, but years would pass before we had that opportunity. Pat always wanted to be with us, too. I liked that my siblings were half-Italian; it gave us more in common. Nevertheless, I felt safe with Roberta—wherever I went on that visit, whatever room I walked into, she was always close behind me and wasn't shy to sit right next to me on the sofa.

My giggles soon turned to tears as I walked into the kitchen and saw my twelve-year-old brother, Orlando. He sat on the counter, covering his face with his hands. I think he was crying, and my tears began to flow and flow. Gosh, how I hated that part of myself! I wanted to stop, to pull myself together, but my tear ducts had a will of their own, and my birth family was unsure of how to respond. They just pretended it wasn't happening and began to chat away. They pulled me into the living room and the next thing I knew I had my sister and mother on either side of me pulling out photo album after photo album, showing me, in pictures, their whole lives: my mother getting married, the growing-up years of the children, holidays, all the normal family stuff, yet to me it was fascinating. I studied each photo, and especially loved the ones of my siblings as babies. They were so cute! I felt immediate connection to both of them, and I also felt surprisingly protective. Suddenly I was taking on the role of big sister, which was so strange after being the youngest in my adoptive family.

I was also shown pictures of great-grandparents and uncles and told about my ethnic heritage. I had Russian, Austrian, and Dutch blood on my birth mother's side, and my father, of course, had been Italian. Wow! No wonder I felt confused at times!

My birth mother went through photos of me as a baby growing up. She had asked me to bring these, but I sensed that for her, looking at them was really painful. I also showed her my adoption file and she read it all. There was a part that showed letters describing my development that were meant for her eyes, but Pat said she had never received them. We concluded that her parents must have kept them from her. She had been given only a single photo of me, which she had kept.

She said that what they had written about my birth father

wanting to marry her was simply not true, that the social services had wanted to make it all look nicer than it was. Maybe that's an English thing, or maybe it made me more acceptable for adoption. After all, who wanted a baby that may have come from bad blood or who might turn out to have too many problems? But I had so needed to believe that my parents wanted to marry each other. It was another fantasy that I had to let go of, and it hurt immensely.

My grandparents soon arrived. My grandfather walked in saying loud hellos and kissing his grandchildren. My grandmother came in quietly behind him. I was still sitting on the sofa with the piles of photo albums, feeling, let's say, a little overwhelmed. He took one look at me and said, "So you're the skeleton in our closet!" What does one say to that? More relatives arrived later that day: the great-uncles who had sheltered my birth mother during her pregnancy, along with their wives, one of whom bought me a welcome present that made me cry again; and my birth mother's brother, the one who had answered the phone the day I had been born and was told "It's a girl." He had kept that knowledge to himself until he had been told about me only a few days before.

Somehow I made it through the afternoon. Luckily, they are a chatty family, so I could sit back and observe. I felt my grandmother staring at me the whole time, yet every time I looked over at her, she looked away. They all told me how much I resembled Pat.

I watched my brother and sister interact with their grandparents and their mother. I could see the shared connection that comes only with years of being a family, years of history with one another, and waves of sadness crashed over me. I would never have that connection with them; those years were truly gone. As Pat had missed watching me grow, I had missed seeing my siblings grow, and I still felt like an outsider. Paradoxically, reunion helped in many ways to fill the void, but in other ways it made the void bigger than ever.

One of my core issues that came up during my pregnancy was "the gap," the space, not feeling like I have a history. It's like the Grand Canyon—a hole in my own identity. So when I would reach back into my memory for that connection with my own mother, I could go back only to when I was nine or ten. I didn't have that primal connection.

—Jacqui

I left that day, as I did many times after our first few meetings, relieved to be alone in my car, to have a break from the bombardment of emotions that came and went. As soon as I had turned the street corner, I began to cry, then howl. A sound like the cry of a wounded animal exploded from me. It was powerful and terrifying, yet I knew that howl had been buried deep within me since the day Pat gave me away. Somehow the heart remembers even when the undeveloped brain cannot. The devastation of losing my mother, the grief that went unhealed, here it all was, overtaking me like the floodwaters from a broken dam. I wanted to see them, to be with my family, yet when I was with them, I felt as though the pain would drown me.

Overwhelmed

I was invited out to dinner to celebrate Pat's and her husband's wedding anniversary. Roberta and Orlando and Pat's brother and his wife picked me up. We all met at a Japanese restaurant. Each table had a little cooker upon which the waiter prepared our food as he showed off his culinary skills: he held the cooking oil way above his head and poured it slowly into a tiny pot, then cut vegetables at great speed, which I found highly irritating.

Wine was ordered. Normally that would not have bothered me, but that night it was very difficult. It wasn't that I wanted to drink—I just didn't want to be around the smell, to observe the subtle (and sometimes not so subtle) changes that come over people as they drink. I felt vulnerable and alone, and longed to be sitting with my recovery friends having a cup of tea and a laugh within the safety of that circle.

One of the presents that my brother and sister gave to their parents was a specially framed photo of themselves when they were small. I felt the ominous welling of tears. Yet again I was reminded that they were connected and I was not. Once more I felt the deep sadness at not having known my siblings as young children, that those years were gone, and that I had missed their lives.

At that moment the waiter began to cook in alcohol the food I had ordered. He was pouring it on, and when I told him that I didn't want alcohol on my food, he assured me it would burn off. He poured more on; again I told him I didn't want it. The rest of the family told me it was no big deal, that I wouldn't taste it. I was in only my second year of sobriety and still scared of the power of alcohol—I didn't want it near me, so I mustered all my strength to repeat that I didn't want it cooked on my food. Against my will I began to cry and couldn't stop. It was like the flood gates had finally opened and I had no control. I felt the sadness of all the years of not knowing my birth mother, the pure loss, the lack of connection to either of my families, the sorrow of missing my brother and sister, the pain of sitting together finally and them being strangers to me. The tears kept falling even though I shouted inside my head, "Stop! It's enough already!" Everyone at the table carried on talking as if it wasn't happening. They, too, were embarrassed by what was happening to me. Pat asked me once if I was okay. Finally I made it to the bathroom, locked myself in, and howled. I wanted to leave right then but I had no car and no money.

Pat found me. She had assumed it was all about the waiter not listening to me, but I couldn't find the words to explain; there was just too much. Finally, I persuaded them to drop me home, and the relief I felt upon entering my flat was overwhelming—I was safe.

The next morning, Pat called to say, "Thanks a lot for ruining my evening." I was devastated, and for me the relationship was never the same again.

I tried to explain the loss I felt, how overwhelmed I was. She replied, "What about me? Didn't you think it was hard for me? The past is over. Let's be happy now we are all together, let's just get on with the future and enjoy now."

I wish it could have been that simple, but it wasn't. For awhile I tried to fake it, but those feelings kept rising up within me as I began to get in touch with things I didn't know were there.

> *I feel my adopted mother had as big a loss as I did, that I wasn't who she really wanted as a daughter.*
>
> *—Lily*

There have been two times when communication was broken off for extended periods, once for two years and the other for a year. Both times each of us wanted the other to understand where we were coming from. We each needed the other to take away the pain and we couldn't, which only made us angrier with one another. Perhaps we were angry too that, instead of a fairy-tale happy ending, meeting each other only brought up feelings made more potent by having been stuffed down for so long. We were both victims of circumstance, and I was crushed that she couldn't be the mother I had dreamed about. It had been just another fantasy.

Making Connections

One month after meeting my birth mother, a very dear childhood friend gave birth to her first child, a daughter. I was very excited and, as soon as I got the telephone call, drove immediately to the hospital. I burst into the room, about to deliver congratulations and a big hello when I abruptly had to change pace: calmness enveloped me, and with it, the energy and peace that only a newborn can bring into the world. I was unsure of what to say and felt like an intruder. My friend's mother sat in a chair watching her new granddaughter. My friend and her husband were on the bed, Gina lying down and David sitting next to her. The baby lay between them. Although they glanced up for a moment to greet me, they were clearly mesmerized and returned their attention to the baby. They imitated the face she made as she tried to focus on her new surroundings, they touched her face and hands, inspecting her all over, as though they couldn't believe that she was real.

All this time I stood quietly by the bed, half hidden by the curtain that they had now pulled back. I, too, just watched. Unexpectedly, tears began to surface along with an ache in my chest. The lightness of my mood began to vanish. I tried to make conversation with Gina's mother, but felt she was just being kind, that secretly she felt I was intruding on a sacred time for the family. I wanted to leave straight away, but waited a while in case they thought I was acting strangely. When I could contain myself no longer, I left, saying I would return in a day or so.

I walked quickly to the elevator and out of the hospital, relieved when I found my little blue car waiting for me. I started the engine and was ready to pull away when I stopped and pulled up the brake. A howl erupted from my throat, tears flowed as though they had no end. I was both unaware and uncaring of whether anyone saw me or not.

At last I began to make the connection, a feeling both uncertain and familiar: my own birth had been nothing like what I just witnessed—no joy, no celebration, no awe. Just a frightened lonely girl and an infant who would soon be parted from her.

Breaking the Silence

I was, as I have said,

Before I got pregnant, I don't recall thinking very much about my birth mother. Having my own children made me realize how horrible it must have been for her. Whenever I see the children's book, "Are You My Mother?", I feel a real sense of loss and sadness. I would advise abortion rather than relinquishment under the closed-records system.

—Kathryn

twenty-four-years old at the time of my reunion, but emotionally I was very young, still carrying all my childhood feelings around my adoption. At that time, I had no support from any professionals in the adoption field.

When I found my birth mother, I was too afraid to tell any of my adoptive family. I kept it to myself, sharing what I was going through only with close friends. Everything felt so overwhelming, so extreme, so powerful and, at times, debilitating, that I could deal with only one stage at a time. I remembered the times my adoptive mother had told me she would help me search, but that she would be hurt if I did. Other times when we discussed my adoption, I felt she was waiting for me to show that I wasn't really interested.

For two years I stayed silent, sometimes visiting both families on the same day, especially if it was a holiday. Each time, I felt the burden of a secret life, but I was crippled with fear. I simply couldn't find the strength to tell them. In fact, I had sworn to my friend Simon, who was helping me, that I would never ever tell them, that it would devastate them, and that they didn't need to know. Yet as time went on, it became harder and harder to juggle my double life, and I was haunted by guilt. What if they found out from somebody else?

I became more aware of my feelings about being adopted after [my babies] were born. I had suppressed them for many years, and having children of my own made me confront them and finally start saying that I was entitled to those feelings. Before, I had always worried about everyone else's feelings and pushed aside my own.

—*Maggie*

At last, about two years after my reunion with my birth mother, I had another revelation: I was driving over to see my adoptive family when it suddenly struck me that my terrible fear wasn't all about me protecting them. The truth was I was terrified that they would reject me, that they would no longer want me as their daughter. I was a grown woman of twenty-six, yet feeling just like that vulnerable child again.

The following Sunday morning I awoke knowing that today was the day. I don't know why it happened that particular day—somehow my body just couldn't contain the secret anymore. I needed to be free from it. I spoke to Simon and he said, "Well, it seems like you can't wait another day. You need to do it now. It will be okay."

My emotions were overwhelming and the tears wouldn't stop. Once again, I was a young child with no anchor. Trembling with an adrenalin rush, I called my parents and told them through my tears that I had to come over and tell them something. I was barely able to speak.

Now I feel so badly over the way I handled it. My parents were so worried. They had no clue, and they later told me their imaginations conjured up all kinds of terrible things. I drove straight over, praying for God's help all the way. I found my parents waiting by the window, looking extremely anxious. The moment I walked in, I blurted it out, "I found my birth mother!"

No one said much at first, but eventually my mother began to ask questions. I told them I had known Pat for a while. They were surprised and didn't understand why I hadn't told them sooner, and why now? Why was I so upset? I didn't know how to answer because I couldn't tell them the truth: that I remembered every incident, every word, every look from my adoptive mother when the subject had come up during my childhood, and that even though we hadn't discussed it in years, her reluctance had affected me deeply. The fact that I was now an adult didn't make any difference to my feelings. I kept silent.

My mother asked to see pictures and I showed them. It felt very strange. Even though my blood family was so connected to me, there was no similarity between the two families. Pat was almost a different generation from my adoptive parents—sixteen years younger—and their lifestyles were not at all similar.

Mum asked about my birth father. I told them the story

and that he was Italian, to which my mother replied, "Yes, we know he was."

I felt as if I had been hit in the pit of my stomach with a bowling ball. My head began to swim. "You knew?" I whispered. I couldn't believe they had known yet never told me. I felt so much anger and shock, yet again I just sat and stared at the floor in silence. Then I noticed that my father, too, was sitting the same way, silently staring down to the floor. He hadn't uttered one word.

I left their house that night feeling very different from before I arrived. I was exhausted and relieved, yet more importantly, I felt more grounded, like I was finally stepping into my own body. It felt good. At last I had done it! The secret was out and I knew then that how my parents chose to deal with this information was up to them. I simply couldn't carry it all anymore; I had to stop protecting their feelings. They were, after all, grownups. It was time for me to heal my sadness and anger, to stop being a victim to this situation, to move on with my life.

CHAPTER NINE

America

I was twenty-eight years old, and had finally reached a place within myself where I was happy with my life. I had recently moved out of my little bedsit into a new flat with low rent that would be mine for as long as I wished. It gave me a feeling of security that I hadn't had before.

I signed up for a foundation course on the history of art, something I had always been interested in, and carried on with my writing and singing. In addition to performing regularly with my own band, I also had another rather strange job: I sold Grassmen at Camden Market. These were a new phenomenon and they quickly became immensely popular. Grassmen were basically dolls made of tights that were filled with sawdust and grass seed. They had whimsical faces and eyeglasses, and all the owner had to do was water them for a few days. When the grass began to grow, these little men were quite irresistible. My friend David for whom I sold them, made them cheaply and sold them cheaply, and customers went nuts. I sold literally hundreds and, as Christmas approached, I would be sold out before the evening. I enjoyed working in the market and meeting so many different types of people.

At last I had stopped obsessing over whether I would marry and start my own family. There were so many other things I could do with my life, and realized I would rather be alone than in a crazy relationship. Nevertheless, I was exhausted with the burden of keeping so many secrets for so many years and constantly protecting my adoptive family and my birth family so that nobody got hurt.

I had a friend named Shelly who had moved to California some years earlier, and we kept in touch. She encouraged me to move on with my life and come to California for a visit. I had no obligations to hold me back, so why shouldn't I take a vacation? The idea of being far away from home exhilarated me.

I arrived in Los Angeles in December 1993, and Shelly met me at the airport. What a dramatic change! I'd left London in the fog and cold, and stepped off the plane onto what might have been a different planet. The sun sparkled and everywhere I looked, flowers bloomed. I couldn't believe how spacious it all seemed and how clean. The sky was so big and there were so many palm trees. Of course I wanted to do all the tourist things that people do when they first visit the West Coast.

A few days into my trip, I was sitting with a group of people I had just met. We were talking about England and they were asking me about life over there. Everyone was ever so friendly and welcoming. The room began to fill up with men and women of all ages, chatting and moving their chairs to get comfortable, when in marched a man carrying a box of literature for the meeting. He wore clown pants and a T-shirt and he was extremely loud. My first thought was, "Who the hell does he think he is? And why is he wearing those ghastly trousers? What egos these Americans have!"

After the meeting, Clown Pants came over and shook my hand. "I'm Jonathan," he said warmly. As I looked into his eyes, I saw a certain gentleness there. Suddenly, I felt that I knew him, that we had met before. The group decided to go out to dinner and I was invited along. We ended up at Bob's Big Boy, a very old and famous burger place on Riverside in Toluca Lake. "Wow!" I thought, "A real American diner, just like in *Twin Peaks*." Jonathan ended up next to me, and I placed my bag between us. "Don't worry," he said with a smile and a twinkle in his eye, "you're safe sitting with me."

At first, I listened as everyone else talked. Then they asked me questions about London and what life was like there. They were a merry bunch, people enjoying life, and I realized how serious we all could be at times back home. Life could indeed be fun—it was something to celebrate! I, too, wanted to laugh and relish my freedom. Right then and there I knew I needed to spend more time with these people. Mark, for instance, had a strong spiritual belief that I wanted to hear more about. There were quieter personalities as well, who were equally committed to trying out life in a new way. The main thread that ran through all my new acquaintances was that enjoying life was a God-given right. And did these people know how to laugh! They offered precisely the kind of spiritual nourishment I had been missing.

I also knew that I wanted to get to know this American, Jonathan, more.

Moving Forward

Two weeks later, I had to go back to London. I didn't want to leave, but I was armed with new ideas to take to my friends and a new attitude I wanted to hang onto. I didn't want to fall back into the negativity that still cropped up for me from time to time. I also wanted to nourish the hope that I had been exposed to. It would be so easy to fall back into the old ways again, and that scared me. That was the road to destruction, and I had to keep moving forward.

I had already decided to return to LA and spend more time there, but first I had to tie up a few things back home and earn some money. During my time back in London, I kept in regular contact with all my new friends, including Jonathan. I was convinced that he would forget about me the moment I left for London, so I was always surprised when he called.

For six months, I worked as hard as I could, waitressing, babysitting, anything to make some money. My closest girlfriend, Carol, told me later that I never really came back to London, that she could see I was already gone, and that no matter how often I said I would be back in a year, she knew that I wouldn't.

Leave-taking has always been extremely difficult for me, even if there is no tension in the parting. The pain of separating reactivates that first, primal separation, and it is something I still battle with. It is hard to trust that, even though we separate, I really will see loved ones again, will still share their closeness, that they will always remember me.

Leaving my family and friends to return to California brought all those feelings churning to the surface once again. At that time, I had never revealed to anyone how deeply saying good-bye affected me—I didn't understand it very well myself and fought it ferociously. But at the airport when all my adoptive family and friends came to see me off, I fell apart. I knew my life was going to change dramatically, and even though we had our problems, they were my family and would be there for me in whatever ways they could.

Mum handed me a beautiful letter telling me how much she would miss me and loved me. It was very healing. She knew I wasn't coming back, something I also knew in my gut, but couldn't face it right then. I cried all the way to LA, which was very embarrassing, as I was seated next to an elderly American couple who thought what I needed was a nice chat about what America was like. I did my best to control my inexhaustible sobs, but they soon gave up and I was left to weep in peace.

Culture Shock

Arriving in LA was suddenly terribly scary. This time, I wasn't going to be there for just two weeks. I had decided to stay a year, and that suddenly felt like an extremely long time. There were major challenges, like where I was going to live and how I would earn a living. At first, I stayed with a friend. (Later, I moved into an empty condo, and finally shared a small apartment with a flat mate.) Getting work was going to be harder than I'd thought, and not having the support of my old recovering friends around me sent me at times into a paralyzed fear.

There was also the culture-shock factor: I began to realize

that speaking the same language didn't mean there weren't quite a few differences between the Americans and the English. We are brought up so differently. Americans are much more patriotic, take a more open view of life, and seem to talk more openly and easily. Total strangers actually said, "Hello," as I walked past them on the street, something that rarely happened in a big city like London. I was always surprised when someone said a big cheery "Good morning!" I was used to being ignored and avoiding eye contact.

Then, of course, there were the basic everyday difficulties, such as the first time I tried to post a letter and couldn't work out where the slot was on the post box. I found myself walking round and around, quite baffled as to how to get the letter sent, when I finally figured it out that you had to lift the handle! I felt so embarrassed, convinced that dozens of people had been watching me and thought me a total imbecile.

The accent caused a difficulty, too. No one seemed to understand when I asked for a glass of "water," and it took me time to feel comfortable saying the word with an American accent. One time I was terribly thirsty, and I took the four-year-old boy whom I was taking care of into a shop with me. I asked for a bottle of water and no one understood. I mimicked water coming out of a tap. The man stared blankly. Finally, I looked down at my little charge and said, "Please help me. Can you tell him what I need?"

"Sure," he said. "She wants water." I got my drink.

Connecting with people had never been easy for me, so all these minor obstacles didn't help. However, they did serve as a good excuse to separate myself when I wanted to. I was in a new place and I was scared. I couldn't busy myself with phone calls and socializing or walking the busy streets of London. I was on my own a lot and began feeling very vulnerable.

Making a Life

One of my new American friends organized a group that

regularly visited a local AIDS hospice, and one day she asked me to come with them and sing. I was happy to be asked but more than a little nervous. Still, I went ahead and at the end of the evening, I had signed up to join the group. Hospice became part of my weekly life, and on the days when I was most homesick and feeling alone, I would visit my patients. Always coming away with a deep sense of gratitude for what I had. It was incredibly fulfilling to participate in this group and I remained a regular until the hospice was closed a year later.

I also began to gather some musicians together to start playing in LA. I hung out with all my new friends, including Jonathan, as much as possible. We would all sit in Jonathan's new house and chat into the small hours as we got to know one another. Jonathan and I were rarely left alone together; there seemed to be safety in numbers.

It was during these informal social gatherings that more of my "stuff" began to surface. My new friends asked questions about my life. I told them I was adopted and that I had met my birth mother. As I began to talk about it and saw that they were truly listening intently, I felt such emotion rise into my chest that I was about to break down. If I let my feelings out, it would be loud and ugly and I would have no control. This felt very uncomfortable, especially since I was trying to impress a man. My new friends would look at me, waiting for more explanation, and I would get up and run out of the room, leaving them to puzzle over what had happened and where I had gone. As for me, I couldn't explain what was going on inside or what it was connected to. All I knew was that the feelings seemed so overwhelming that I thought I would fall apart.

This happened a few times. I had never felt emotions on that level before, and didn't trust anyone enough to let them see these feelings surface. Nevertheless, I began to get an inkling of how much unresolved stuff I still had to deal with. Miss Recovery wasn't as recovered as she had hoped.

Romance the Old-fashioned Way

Jonathan and I went for long drives in the mountains. It was very romantic, and we would talk for hours. Jonathan showed me all of LA. We went to the movies a lot, something we both enjoyed. Nevertheless, we decided not to become lovers, to just get to know each other as friends. For me, sex always clouded my reality. Once it was brought into the equation, the relationship was either over or based solely on sex, and I had promised myself not to do that again. So for the first time, I tried to get to know Jonathan, to see who he really was and to allow him to see me, warts and all. I had never stayed around long enough to do that before. Yet who would have thought that just sitting and being with someone you cared about could bring up so many intense feelings—mainly fear? For the first time, I began to see my fear of intimacy. I had no idea how to be authentic, to behave without the sexual lure. I had always pointed my finger at the man, saying he was the one who was unable to commit, when the truth was it was I who couldn't.

As I've said earlier, I felt from the beginning that Jonathan and I had known each other before, a feeling that Jonathan shared. We both realized we had never actually met yet there was something strangely familiar about him that I found comforting. I felt drawn to his enthusiasm for life, his spirit. We began to discover that we shared similar interests, that we both wanted certain things in life, but mainly that our spiritual paths had to come first. We also had a lot of fun.

It became easy to see that Jonathan liked me for *me*. It was incredibly liberating and I am so grateful that he, too, by this point in his life, had had enough casual encounters. Up until then, naive and immature as I was, I had based my whole romantic life on sexual attraction. What I learned is that in married life sex is only a small part of the package.

Commitment

When Jonathan began to talk about marriage, I freaked out and said, "I can't get married."

"Why not?" he asked. "Do you have a secret husband you've forgotten to tell me about?" I laughed nervously and said, "I just couldn't."

Jonathan managed to look confused and amused at the same time. And I had no idea why I thought I couldn't get married.

Eventually he gave up talking about it, although he did wonder out loud whether I wanted to spend my life flitting form one relationship to another without truly committing or take the risk. *Ouch.* That hurt. I knew it was true, yet I was terrified. I wasn't even sure of what.

Gradually, I truly began to trust Jonathan, something I'd never felt with a man before. That was extremely important to me. I cannot say specifically how it happened. I just watched how he lived his life. He was consistent with me, he kept promises as best he could, and was gentle and kind—not only to me but to others. Naturally, like everyone else, he had his dark side, but it didn't seem to bring him down. He could snap out of a bad patch, and his view would always turn to the positive. That was something I wanted; I liked that he trusted life's process. I wanted to strive for that, to know not just in my head, but deep inside that it was okay to enjoy life. In fact, it is a crime not to.

Most important, he made me feel loved. That indeed is an incredibly healing gift. I had been so afraid to let my defenses down, to feel love or be loved, and knew that really I was lonely and wanted to share my life with another person. And here he was. I wasn't going to let fear sabotage my chance at happiness.

We got engaged in December 1994, and that's when I started acting out more of my adoption stuff. Poor bloke, Jonathan must have thought he was going to marry a psycho. We would have a lovely day together and then I would create some argument and tell him to leave. In fact, I remember pushing him away, saying, "Just leave, you are going to sooner or later, so why don't we just get it over with?" He took a lot, he tells me now, because he knew I was just scared. He deserves a medal for bravery and tolerance.

Moving in with him was hard. I remember asking him if we could change some pictures around, which at first he didn't take to kindly, because they were his beloved car photos. But I didn't want them in every room of the house. We had a debate but soon worked out an agreement. Nevertheless, I felt terrified that he would ask me to leave because it wasn't really my house, that I should be grateful he'd been willing for me to move in. I began to remember having the same feeling as a child. If I clashed with my parents, I worried they would send me back to the adoption agency.

CHAPTER TEN

Marriage, Moving, and Motherhood

I have heard it said many times that the most stressful events in life are marriage, moving, having babies, and divorce, so I decided to choose three of those major life changes in a very short space of time. First, we got married in London. At the same time, we packed up my flat. It was a terribly exciting time, yet scary and painful, as well. Separating from my family brought on something akin to panic. The way I dealt with it was by not actually saying goodbye to England, telling myself that for now we were going to live in America, but that we might be back in London at any time.

I was very glad to change my name to Jonathan's. As an adoptee, I had grown up with a name I liked very much, but always knew that really wasn't who I was. I was somebody else— I just didn't know who. After meeting my birth mother, I knew half my genetic lineage, but to this day, the paternal half is a mystery. So my surname never gave me a feeling of wholeness because it really wasn't who I was. I have heard parents say, "That's my boy! He is a Smith down to the ground." Or "She's my daughter all right, just like my side of the family." Well, I didn't feel like anybody's side of the family. I just felt a huge gap inside. So taking on a new name felt wonderful. For the first time I could be who I really was, that I belonged to this name, that my own family was going to start now.

The Wedding

My wedding day is indeed a memory I will treasure forever. Mum did an incredible job. It was really important that we get married in England. I wanted all my friends and family with me, especially my childhood and recovering friends, because they knew where I had come from and they had been so supportive.

Since Jonathan and I were of different religions, we got married in a registry office, something like a justice of the peace in America. It was in a beautiful, very old brick building surrounded by gardens. It also featured a large driveway with plenty of room for the wedding car to drive up. Normally in a registry-office wedding, the entire wedding party has to wait outside and walk in together, but I so wanted to walk in last. As it was a quiet day of the week (Tuesday, July 4, 1995), my husband-to-be and his friends (who had flown over to be his best men and support) spoke to the official ladies and asked if I could enter last so that Jonathan would not see me ahead of time. At first they were a little flustered and in awe of these handsome Americans. They said they couldn't promise, but just then a friend of mine, who was a popular television actress, arrived. The ladies were so excited to meet her that they soon made a place for me to hide so Jonathan and I shouldn't see each other.

I waited in a small office with my dear friend Carol, my dad, and a little girl for whom I'd babysat. My grand entrance was so much fun. Even though it was not a religious service, the love of all the people I cared about filled the room with a beautiful spiritual presence. After the ceremony, we went off to dinner and dancing. On each table there were British and American flags. What a fine time we had!

Part of me wished that my birth family could have been there too, but it would have been too hard for my parents, and I didn't want that day spoiled with strained feelings. In an ideal world, both my families would have come together.

Honeymoon

When I tell you what happened on our honeymoon, you (the reader) will undoubtedly think I am certifiable. Yet perhaps one of you has had a similar experience.

We took our honeymoon in Stratford-upon-Avon—Shakespeare land—which for Jonathan was very exciting as he felt a great infinity with the playwright. Stratford is a magical place. The streets, the houses, and all the countryside surrounding them are incredibly beautiful, and there is so much to see. We explored almost every part of the town, visiting museums and Shakespeare's house. We even sat together on the bench where Will and his girlfriend, Anne Hathaway, had sat when they were courting.

One afternoon as we walked along a canal, I suddenly had the strongest feeling of being pregnant. I actually wasn't, but I spent the whole day in a state of exquisite warmth, as though surrounded and protected inside a bubble. I existed in another dimension apart from all the hundreds of people walking past me. My belly felt full, and I experienced a contentedness I had never known. I wanted the feeling to last forever, and was almost embarrassed to tell Jonathan, who always became slightly nervous when I mentioned babies. He wasn't quite ready at the time, and wanted to do the provider bit of having money and a job—all the sensible things.

The next day, as we walked through the town of Stratford-upon-Avon, a total stranger rushed up to us and gave us tickets for a bus tour. He was unable to use them, and would we like them? We thanked him profusely and he disappeared back into the crowded street. When we looked at the tickets, there were actually three of them. Later the same day, we went into a museum. The man at the ticket counter became irritated when three tickets instead of the two we requested popped out of the machine. "This has never happened to me before," he said.

We had decided before we got married that we would wait about a year before starting a family. On the plane back to America we whittled it down to six months. But once we got home, the visitations, as I like to call them, became even stronger. I had a constant feeling that Jonathan and I weren't alone anymore, that there was someone else present. The feeling got so intense that I could wait no more. I told Jonathan as we were driving home in LA that I felt, right then and there, as if an entity, a powerful energy, were in my womb and that this baby was so ready that I was finding it hard to argue. But I wanted Jonathan to be ready too; I wanted him to want the baby as much as I did. Our baby had to be consciously desired by both of us, conceived with a mutual commitment, not a surprise or the result of a careless night of passion. Jonathan listened quietly, taking in everything I said.

A week later, my husband told me he had felt the baby around him, too, and that he was now ready. Suddenly I panicked. I'd never been pregnant before. What if I couldn't conceive? Jonathan looked at me gently and said, "Zara, I feel like if I breathed on you, you would get pregnant." He was right. I was pregnant six weeks after the wedding.

My adoptive mother and father were unable to conceive, which is how my brother and I came to be part of their family. Without being conscious of the origin, I spent most of my life feeling certain I would also be unable to conceive. So when my husband and I decided to make a baby, I knew it would take years, and we would probably need infertility therapy. We began our effort with no real serious plan—I wasn't taking basal temperatures or charting my cycles or consulting the moon. We thought we would try for six months and if nothing had happened, then worry. I got pregnant within two months and it really threw me. I was totally unprepared emotionally. Wow! I am fertile.

—Nicole

The Gifts of Motherhood

Motherhood is an incredible miracle. What I didn't expect is how it has awakened parts of me that were long dormant or perhaps not even there to begin with. Mainly it has gotten me in touch with the most terrifying emotions I, as an adoptee, could ever experience: love, intimacy, and the inevitable that will one day happen in some form or another, loss. I had never before allowed myself to really love. It is true that I fell deeply in love with my husband, but I can always find ways within my marriage of keeping distance, putting up walls. With my beautiful children this has been impossible. I have never loved with such tenacity or felt such depth of emotion, nor had I ever before been in touch with the true effects of my adoption; mainly feelings of loss and sadness that I had suppressed my entire life. It seems that birthing my children was also a birth for my whole self.

On the night our first child was conceived, I knew instantly I was pregnant. Later, though, I was assailed by doubt. I had terrible cramping in my stomach and went to a midwife for a blood test, but it came back

When I nursed and cared for my babies—especially my firstborn—I felt that I was in some way nurturing my own baby self, the one whom no one had welcomed to the world with love.

—Octavia

negative. I was so upset! I had felt so sure. A few days later while Jonathan was out, I did a home test and was so nervous I ended up peeing all over the stick and dropping it down the toilet. I decided to wait until he returned home and was outside working on his car. This time doing it the right way, I waited, holding my breath, and clear enough, two pink lines appeared. At that point I felt as though I'd flown out of my body. Jonathan tells me I came floating out of the house, waving the stick and muttering that I thought I was pregnant but wasn't really sure. Could he check it just in case? He came in the house very quickly, took one look at the two pink lines, and declared, "You're pregnant!"

"Are you sure?" I asked.

He pointed to the picture on the box and then at the stick, which by this point had two deep red lines that looked liked they had been drawn on with indelible marker. "Two lines," he said patiently, pointing at the diagram and looking at me as if I couldn't speak English. "Two lines," he repeated emphatically, pointing at the stick. "Watch my lips, Zara. You are pregnant and I have no job and the car won't start!" We both stopped and caught our breath. We were pregnant. We were ecstatic.

I did another test later that day and then another first thing the next morning, "Just in case," I explained to Jonathan.

"In case what?" he asked.

"In case it goes away," I said lamely

I booked an appointment with my doctor, who said he would do a blood test to be sure, but that the home tests were pretty accurate. They came back positive. I finally began to believe that, yes, I was really was pregnant. That I, Zara, an adoptee, was able to get pregnant and have my own child. I had never felt that would be allowed.

Pregnancy

I wasn't working at the time of my pregnancy, just waiting for my immigration papers to come through. I couldn't actually leave the country, and that left me very uneasy. What if something should happen to my family and I couldn't go home? Getting married to an American was not as straightforward as I had thought. There was a lot of red tape, and we had to wait a year-and-a-half for our interview to prove that our marriage was legal.

I spent much of my time rehearsing with a band and writing songs. I had a lot to say, and it became a joke when every week I turned up with another new song. "Wow," my bass player would say, "you really are on a roll with this pregnancy thing."

I felt very homesick during this time and didn't as yet have many friends. Nevertheless, being alone was good for me in lots of ways. I couldn't run—I had to sit with my feelings and examine them. Pregnancy is a strange state of being. The first time, for me, was so daunting because—let's face it—you have absolutely no idea what is going to happen or how you're going to feel. Yet at the same time, once I knew I was pregnant, it felt completely right. Somehow, everything I had ever done in my life made sense because it had led me to this place of marriage and pregnancy.

Everything else seemed totally irrelevant.

Being a fearful person, I like to control everything—I mean *everything*. How other people feel, what is going to happen next year, how to keep everyone happy and liking me. I have been known to take great risks so I can maintain the illusion of being in control. Then I got pregnant and lo and behold! I had absolutely no say in any of it. My tummy began to expand; I began to crave oranges and muffins and went to great lengths to make sure I had my supply. As a veteran of various addictions, I was very good at feeding my needs and spent many wonderful hours in the Aroma Café, downing blueberry muffins and taking a few home.

I enjoyed the changes in my body and marveled at the fact that this little being knew just how to grow. At the appropriate number of weeks, he grew toes and toenails and little fingers. How did he know how to do that? I realized that in spite of what I ate or thought, my baby was just going to keep on growing until the day he decided to be born. There was nothing I could do to persuade him to come out any sooner.

As an adoptee about to become a mother, I had no real idea that this state was like standing on the edge of an active volcano. A fountain of lava was about to erupt from its depths, spilling out all its contents with no warning. Four months earlier, I had started therapy with a counselor, an adoptee herself specializing in adoption work. Thank goodness for her.

I began to read everything I could find on adoption. It amazes me that prior to starting therapy, I had never read anything on adoption. It must have been my way of believing the myth that I was really okay. After all, I had two parents, and had been told often enough how lucky I was, how grateful I should be. Yet I felt guilty because I didn't always feel grateful; just sad and I didn't know why. It is rare for anybody to say to an adoptee, "It must be so hard for you that you were given away," or "You must miss and wonder about your mother."

My therapist gave me great reading materials and

suggestions (see the Suggested Reading List at the back of this book). I was so hungry to read them that I could barely wait to get home and would attempt to read them while driving, then howl all the way home—not very advisable on the LA freeways.

Feelings, more intense and more primal than anything I'd experienced before, began to stir deep within me. They were somehow familiar, and the tears and grief, which I had carried for so long, felt almost comforting. I was a few months pregnant when I started having experiences of what I later learned was my own birth. They would often happen in the night. I would wake up and feel as though an entity was trying to leave my body. It was like a huge round boulder that crept up slowly from somewhere deep within. Then it would begin to try and spiral out of me. I tried to ignore it, but it felt as if I was going to burst open. I would sit up in bed and begin to cry softly. Then, as the energy of the boulder reached my throat, my voice would go higher and higher and louder and louder and I would feel myself whizzing through a long tunnel. Tremendous fear would overwhelm me every time I saw the end. I'd get up and pace around, saying, "No, no, I am not ready for this," never allowing myself to pass through to the other side. For if I did, I would surely die.

Jonathan would wake up and somehow figure out what was going on. Then he would hold me, which was hard for me to allow him to do. I'd lean backwards on him and he would reassure me, telling me it was safe to go through what I needed to, that I would be okay. Today he tells me that the sounds he heard were like those of a baby. For me, it was intense and frightening because the sounds were so primal. During these episodes, I had no control, yet each time it happened, I would try to go a little further.

I phoned my therapist. "Is this normal?" I asked, a little embarrassed. She assured me that even though it wasn't common, it did sometimes happen. She advised me to allow the process to develop. It even had a name: *cellular memory*. The body remembers experiences from before we even have words. I thought it was going to kill me.

Further along in my pregnancy, I began to have dreams of birth. I never actually saw myself give birth, however. It was always the next day, and I'd show up at the hospital, walk up to the nurse's station and tell them I had come to collect my baby, but I had no idea what my baby looked liked or what sex it was.

Pregnancy is a vulnerable time for women. I worried the whole way through; always thinking I would either lose the baby or that there would be something wrong with him. I just couldn't grasp that I, like thousands of generations of women before me, could give birth at the end of nine months. You may call it self-obsession, and in a way it was. I believed that for me it would be different, that it wouldn't be a normal experience, that something would go wrong.

I regularly met other pregnant women at an exercise class. We would chat about our visits to the OB while we awkwardly mounted bicycles and pedaled as best we could with our expanding bellies. "My baby is huge, I hope I can get it out," or "I can't stop eating chocolate! I have put on fifty pounds, and I'm only seven months pregnant." And then hysterical laughter as one of us tried to get up from the floor after doing our Kegels. It was fun, but I often found myself studying these women, looking for signs of their feelings. Nobody mentioned her fears, and I wanted desperately to tell them how I felt, that the reason I was extra tired that day

Three of my friends were pregnant the same time as I was. I was convinced theirs would be healthy and mine would be deformed. I was afraid for the whole pregnancy. Right after my child's birth, I began to search [for my birth mother] for the first time.
—Paula

I was fearful my whole pregnancy that I would have a disabled child.
—Rachel

was because I had been up for a couple of hours rebirthing and howling the night before. But I didn't feel I could throw that into general conversation, so I just smiled my way through the classes and kept everything hidden.

One day at the end of class, one of the women finished a chat with a woman who appeared to be in her late thirties. She had just had a baby, but she didn't seem like it. She was a little distant and there was none of the elation or joy that I would have expected from a woman who had just given birth. After she left, the other woman turned to the rest of us and said, "That woman did the most selfless act a human being could do."

We all looked at her expectantly. "She gave her baby to her brother because his wife couldn't have children. Isn't that wonderful? He is so happy."

I felt as though ice water had been poured down my back. Everyone else agreed, while I suddenly felt sick to my very core and intensely angry. In the space of a second, I went through a maelstrom of feeling for that poor baby. I wanted to shout, "You are all nuts! What about that baby? Have you considered how he might be feeling? Don't you know that it's going to affect his whole life? How could she do such a thing?"

But I never uttered a word, just walked away, leaving the girls still talking. "What we need are more women in the world like her."

Birth

I had just finished watching *Seven,* about a psychopath who kills everybody and delivers the head of Brad Pitts' girlfriend to him in a box. Do not ask me why, at nine months pregnant, I chose to watch that movie. There was still a week before my due date but I had drunk castor oil, as I had heard it would help get the baby moving. I decided to have a cup of tea and walked into the kitchen. Suddenly water started running down my legs, and I thought, "Oh great! Now I am incontinent." I paged Jonathan and he called back quickly.

"Water keeps coming out of me," I said.

"Your water broke," he replied.

"I don't know—do you think so?" I had gone into a weird space and felt very detached from everything. Jonathan came home immediately and called the hospital. They told him to bring me in straight away. I had had some mild contractions earlier, but now they were becoming stronger. "I don't need to go," I protested. "They will just check me and send me home." Jonathan gave me a strange look but said nothing. Instead, he got the bag, the one they tell you to prepare ahead of time to take to the hospital.

"Why are you getting the bag?" I demanded. "I won't need it."

Jonathan turned to me again. This time he smiled nervously. "Zara, you are going to have a baby."

"I'll bet you I am not today," I said.

He didn't argue. "Get in the car," he said, taking the bag.

"We won't need it," I repeated.

Once at the hospital, they placed a wristband on my arm and admitted me. I glanced at my husband with surprise. He smiled back, knowing that it was in his best interest *not* to say, "I told you so."

Even though Jonathan stayed with me the whole time, I was terrified and it was a long labor. I wanted to go drug-free, but soon began to wonder whether I was brave or just stupid. The baby got stuck and, finally, after three hours of pushing, they suctioned him out. Suddenly, a lot of people came rushing into the room, but I wasn't sure why. The doctor wanted to get the baby breathing, so she didn't hand him to me right away, but I saw that it was a boy. I looked over anxiously to where they were helping him. "Is he okay?" I asked. After what seemed an eon of time, I heard a cry.

"He's fine!" someone reassured me.

Moments later, they handed him to me all wrapped up in a soft little blanket. I stared at his face in awe, and then at Jonathan, whose eyes caught mine and then fastened in amazement on our son. "Hello," I said. "I am your mummy." He stared back.

My son's birth was so gentle and so easy and so beautiful! I couldn't help thinking that someone was looking after me. I'd had a great opportunity and I am no longer the one who is struggling and left behind. It was like the gods came together and said, "You have done all this work and here is our gift."
—Sheila

He's Not Going Anywhere Without Me

At last, he was here, my baby boy! I had felt the whole pregnancy that I was carrying a boy. When looking at baby clothes, I looked only at boys' things, thinking boy's thoughts. I was delighted that my intuition had been right.

While pregnant, I visited a bookshop to look at color pictures of a baby in its mother's womb at different stages. I'd check the appropriate month and stare at that strange-looking creature with bud arms and a large head and would weep right there in the bookshop, imagining my baby and thinking how beautiful he was. I even had a dream that when my baby was presented to me, he was a little monster with two heads and strange eyes. Yet I fell instantly in love with him, and knew then that I would love my baby no matter what.

After a few minutes, the doctors wanted to whisk him off for a bath. I was seized with panic, afraid he would be taken away from me. I told Jonathan to go with them, to hold the baby and never, not even for one instant, take his eyes off him. I said it over and over. My poor husband must have felt like an imbecile, but he was beginning to get an understanding of my irrational fear.

Once Zachary was back from his bath, I was able to relax, and felt a contentedness I had never experienced before. I held him for a long time—and then we decided to count his toes. We all stayed the night in the hospital. Once, the nurses came in and said, "Let us take him to the nursery so you can get some sleep. He's so lovely, the girls will adore him."

"No way," I said. "He's not going anywhere without me." So we spent the night with Zachary asleep on me and I nursed him. I hardly slept; I just wanted to look at him. I couldn't believe he was real. Jonathan and I took turns holding Zachary, dozing off occasionally, and enjoying the privacy of our little hospital room. The next morning we took our son home.

I remember going to the hospital with anxiety and great fear. I wouldn't get out of the car. I said I had to wait for a contraction. Last year, twenty-three years later, I realized I hadn't wanted to go to the hospital because I'd thought they would take the baby away, that I would lose her.

—Treva

Nightmare

I had looked after many children and babies in my life before Zachary came along, so I really believed that mothering wouldn't be that difficult. I felt like I had some understanding of children, but I was in for a big surprise. No matter how much I loved those other children, nothing could have prepared me for the overwhelming feelings that the arrival of my own baby brought. I had had no clue whatsoever, and the power of these emotions was frightening.

I felt so overwhelmed, so inadequate, that I didn't know how to express myself. My psyche, however, appeared to know exactly how. One night when Zachary was about six weeks old, I sat up in bed sweating, shaking, and crying. I had dreamed that Zachary had been taken from me. A strange man grabbed him and ran away. I woke in such a state of confusion that I believed it had really happened. I went into the lounge where Zachary and Jonathan lay sleeping in order to let me rest and saw that Zachary was safe, but I couldn't stop crying.

Jonathan assured me over and over. "It's just a dream, Zara, it's not real!" It took all night for the feeling and visual memory of the nightmare to fade.

That nightmare, the only one I'd had since childhood, was the first of many I suffered in the first few months of my son's life. The theme was always the same: my son was taken from me, sometimes by a man, sometimes a woman, and I searched for him frantically. Always waking before I found him. The depth of grief I experienced in these dreams was what I should imagine a mother would feel if her child had died—they were truly unbearable. I have to say that in my entire sobriety to that point, I had never felt so strongly the need to numb myself. Thankfully, this period passed and my sobriety remained intact. Nevertheless, it has taken me until now (my son is five at the time of this writing) to be able to look back at that time, write about it, and fully experience it without fear.

Snatched Away

With time, I began to realize the origin of those nightmares: as a child, I had continually looked for my mother on every street. I always knew that she was out there; I just didn't know where. It was I who had been snatched away by someone unknown to me.

When my children were younger, I had many nightmares of them getting lost and [me] not being able to find them.

—*Martina*

I could never leave my son, not even for an instant. I would do the normal things that mothers do, checking to see if he was breathing and so on, but what I never told anyone was that I went to his room to make sure he was still there. I always feared that he would just disappear into thin air. Of course, it never made any rational sense—he was in a room with no way of getting out, but I kept checking nonetheless. In the end, I decided to have him with me at all times. I never told Jonathan the truth of the matter until much later. Too afraid that if I revealed too much, I would be sent to a doctor who would find me an incompetent mother and take the baby away.

So there I was, a new wife, a new mother, in a new country, with all this irrational behavior, trying my best not to show people, to keep smiling and be friendly, to appear as if I were a functioning human being. Gosh, it was hard work!

One day when Zachary was only a few weeks old, my husband and I had a silly argument. I was left feeling that Jonathan and Zachary were eyeing me critically. Certain my son was assessing whether or not I was doing well as a mother. I stood apart from them, feeling ganged up against, when Jonathan looked at me and said, "Zara, this is your home. We are not going to throw you out."

I was amazed and wondered, "How did he know that?" I'd spent my whole life growing up waiting for my parents to tell me to leave, and now as an adult woman in my own home, I still felt that eventually they would cast me out, that I didn't have the same rights as everyone else.

Twelve-step programs had literally saved my life, but in California, I discovered adoption support groups,

I had a very intense and strange reaction with my new baby. It was panic at the thought of being separated from him for even a few minutes. I didn't know then that I had been adopted, so my experience was almost the perfect clinical double-blind survey. Now I realize, I was remembering being taken from my own mother. My experience was so much more than panic. I truly relived events as well as the grief and terror of the separation. Even later, when people said it was time (according to them) for me to leave my child with strangers and go back to work, I was crippled by fear at the thought of being separated from him.
—Nancy

It was right after my daughter was born that I started therapy. I began to have nightmares of mass destruction—I was the only one alive. I joined ALMA (Adoptees Liberty Movement Association) and felt for the first time that I wasn't the only adoptee in the world.
— *Veronica*

Becoming a mother has brought up so many feelings about my adoption. I am filled with all the questions about her that I have spent many years not letting myself ask because there are no answers.
— *Patti*

something I had never encountered before. When Zachary was about nine months old, my therapist suggested I attend some meetings of a group called CUB—Concerned United Birthparents. It had been started by a group of birth mothers, but adoptees were welcomed at their meetings. CUB helped me a lot in understanding Pat, but I needed a place where there were just adoptees so that we could talk freely without the worry of hurting anyone's feelings. I, and one of my new friends, started such a group. At last I found people coping with abandonment and loss issues that are specific to adoption, and I felt comfortable just sitting in the same room and listening to other adoptees' stories. I wasn't crazy after all. Adoption is an emotional subject, and the problems don't end with reunion. In some ways, reunion is just the beginning of the road. Pregnancy and childbirth was the route for me to get to the heart of my feelings.

CHAPTER ELEVEN

Mothers, Fathers, and Home

I saw a television program recently involving women who, at an early age, had lost their mothers. The pain and the grief they endured as they grew up were devastating, and their stories truly upset me. The reason I could identify with these woman is that, growing up, I, too, felt like my mother had died. This was horribly conflicting, since after all I had a mother. I never told anyone of these feelings—it would have made no sense whatsoever. The worst part was not knowing if my birth mother was alive or dead, so I lived in a constant state of unresolved grief, always searching for her, as a lot of adoptees do. Though most of the time it was subconscious, I have read that, just as there is no closure for the families of soldiers missing in action, there is no closure for the adoptee.

My adoptive mother mothered me as best she could: she treated me as her own. I in turn loved her. She was the only mother of whom I had any memory. Unfortunately for us both, she didn't know that adopted babies grieve no matter how much you love them, feed them, kiss them, and cuddle them. The adoptive mother is not the mother they want. Through no fault on my mother's part, I never really trusted the relationship. I always felt afraid I would be rejected again, that maybe she didn't really like me, that I wasn't the right daughter for her after all, that if she had had her own biological daughter they would have had a better relationship. It has taken me years to understand the complexities of this issue, and now that I have children of my own, it is becoming clearer than ever what we—my adoptive mother, my birth mother and I—missed out on.

Where Had I Been?

I remember one day showing my adoption file to Carol, who was visiting from England. She was amazed at the content and read it all. When she got to the part about me being sent to a foster mother at two weeks of age, she looked at me with tears in her eyes and said, "Why have you never shown me this before? I had no idea!" I didn't know how to answer. My adoption file wasn't something I showed to people no matter how close they were to me—it was sacred, it was my identity.

I was very touched at Carol's tears and will always be grateful for her reaction. It helped me to get in touch with even more emotions that I had been suppressing. In the past, whenever anyone had expressed sympathy about this issue, I had a difficult time and never seemed to be in touch with my own sadness. But something happened after that day. I read through my file again and began to work out those early weeks: where had I been?

I hesitated so long to have a baby because I was afraid I would be unable to bond with [my child], not because I was adopted per se, but because I had spent the first seven months of my life in the maternity home nursery under conditions of which I had no knowledge. I was very afraid I had been physically damaged in some way.

—Reyna

First, I was with my birth mother, who had intended to keep me for a while. But she had hemorrhaged and required two blood transfusions. So, at only a few days of age, I was separated from her, and a few days after that, I was placed in foster care. On January 4, 1965, I met my adoptive parents and was immediately taken home with them. I was two months old and with my third mother.

When I finished connecting all those dots, it made a huge impact on me, more so because at that time my son was only a year old. I thought about those early weeks with him and how hard it had been for me, how overwhelmed I had felt. I remembered when he first smiled at me, his recognition of me, his mother, how much he had changed and grown and the routine we had established, how we were getting to know each other.

A few days after all this, I lay down for a nap. Suddenly I found myself thinking about my foster mother and I began to howl from that deep place again—another cellular memory experience! There were no words for it, since it emerged from a time before I had language. It came to me with amazing clarity: I was crying for my foster mother—not because it had been a bad time, but because it had been a good time. I wept because I realized I had bonded with her and leaving her had been, once again, devastating.

Guilt

When Zachary was born, my mother came over to visit. He was just six weeks old. This is about the age that many babies are adopted, so for adoptees who are new mothers, a lot of old grief can be triggered. It can be expressed consciously or unconsciously. Subsequently, I was in a very emotional place when my mother visited. Having a baby, as most women know, is the biggest life change one can undergo. In addition, I was having those nightmares and cellular memories that I couldn't put into words; so being around my mother was hard. I wasn't able to express all that I was feeling because I was still trying to protect her. I found myself feeling guilty for being able to have a baby so easily, for being able to breastfeed, and I felt sad for my mother because she had never been able to have the experience of her own child. I began to see that she had missed out greatly— we both had—and there was nothing I could do to change that; I could never be her natural daughter.

> *When I got pregnant, I felt guilty toward my adoptive mother. I was sad that I didn't have my [birth] mother, who could tell me what it was like when she was pregnant [with me]. I heard [such stories] from friends and friends' mothers, and it is definitely a very strong missing piece for me. I think about how my daughter will be pregnant one day and I will be able to tell her what it was like being pregnant with her.*
>
> *—Sally*

Guilt is a strange waste of time in the cold light of day. It made no sense at all to feel guilty for not looking like my mother, for being able to conceive a child. Nevertheless, the guilt had always been there. I just didn't realize it until Zachary was born.

I look at my son and cannot believe how much he looks like my husband. I am told he also looks like me, although that is harder for me to see. I notice how much strangers like to talk about whom the baby looks like, and I'm thrilled when they see the resemblance. But on a deeper level I know him, I understand his stubbornness, his ability to play imaginary games, the way he loves to run fast, his likes and dislikes. I understand when he throws a tantrum—he is so much like me.

"Oh no," I pray to God, "please let him have an easier time than I did. Please let him not take everything so sensitively that he can barley function. Please don't let him believe that he will be forgotten or lost forever. I pray he has more self-esteem than I did." And then I am quieted by a voice that says, "Zara, he knows who his mum and dad are." "Oh yes," I think, "he won't be spending his childhood looking for a stranger who might bear some resemblance to himself."

Persistent Fears

The fears I have about my children being taken go out of control every month or so, still I am learning to stop the scenario and scream, "Go away!" or "F*** straight off and stop ruining my life!"

But my, how they like to persist, especially when everyone is getting along well, and more especially, when I stop in the middle of playing with my children or holding them tightly as they go to sleep. I take in the moment and feel a love that I have never felt for another human being ever. I often tell them how much I love them,

I had a lot of fears and paranoia about my children.
—Violet

I couldn't have anyone babysit my children, only my parents. I had a strong fear of losing them. I still do today, but I am learning to control it.
—Tanya

how happy I am to have them. One night when we were all quiet and relaxed I started to cry just from the feeling, from the joy. My son said, "Mummy, are you crying again?" and he reached over to feel my tears in the dark.

I tried to wipe my eyes quickly, laughing. "I'm crying because I'm happy, because I have never been so happy in my life."

"I don't cry when I'm happy," he replied. And then, "I love you too, Mummy."

Make No Mistake

I am trying hard to change my core belief system, which says, "You are a mistake, you were never meant to be born, and because of that, you deserve nothing." Even though a lot of healing has taken place and many questions have been answered, I continue to struggle with this issue.

One evening when Zachary was barely a few weeks old, I lay on the bed with him. As I gazed down at him, I was struck all over again with a deep sense of wonder at the miraculous quality of the newborn, in awe of his beauty, his sweetness, vulnerability, goodness, and innocence. "You are perfect," I whispered, "just the way you are." As he stared back at me, I was overcome with deep emotion. In that moment I knew that

I, Zara, wasn't a mistake—that no baby could possibly be a mistake; I was meant to be here, to be the mother of this child. For me to keep thinking that I had been a mistake would be a disservice not only to my son, but also to every child on earth.

I have always carried guilt that I have done something wrong, and I spent a lot of my relationships apologizing. Then I finally had my son, and I realized that he couldn't make a mistake at his age. When I met my birth mother, she told me that I had done nothing wrong. That was very powerful.

—Wendy

Missing My Birth Father

I have cried many tears for a man I have never known. I never understood until recently that it's possible to miss what you never had as much as I have—and still do.

Many times as Jonathan, Zachary, and I lay in bed at night, Jonathan would tell me stories of his father. This man contracted Alzheimer's disease when my husband was just a teenager. He died twelve years later, but Jonathan has fond memories of his father and speaks of him often. On one particular night, listening to him talk about his father and then about being a father, I felt a deep pain beginning to rise. I almost felt jealous that, even though he had lost his father, at least Jonathan knew who he was and had been able to spend time with him. I began to cry very deeply and found myself uttering, "I miss my father." The words surprised me, yet it felt so good to finally be in touch with the truth— so freeing to say out loud that I do miss him. I miss not knowing what he looks like, who he is, what kind of man he is, and that although his relationship (if you could call it that) with Pat was fleeting, it doesn't make any difference to me. I still would like to know who he is as much as I wanted to know my birth mother.

For years, I have battled with Pat trying to get information on my birth father. The first few years were very difficult. I could tell she had a lot of anger toward him, and she wasn't helpful to me. She didn't seem to understand how important it was for me to know, how some small, seemingly insignificant memory might help me to savor and imagine what he was like. Pat assured me that she had told me everything she knew, but as time passed, I repeated the same questions. Sometimes I would get a little bit more. I know they went to see a "Carry On" movie the night I was conceived. I have also been told that when Pat informed him she was pregnant, he panicked. A while later, though, he tried to contact her by phone, and she even recalls seeing him on the underground when she was pregnant, but doesn't remember if he saw her or not. She told her mother to tell him to go away. Pat says she wishes now she had spoken to him.

A few years ago, I decided to find the club where my birthparents had met. My girlfriend in London took it upon herself to find the club. It had changed names but was still the same as it had been in the sixties. She sent me photos that I still have. When I went back to visit London, I walked up and down those streets. When I eventually found the club, I couldn't believe it. With my husband and son standing beside me, I peered through the window, pressing my nose against the glass, trying to see inside. I was disappointed because it was closed for refurbishing. Just as we were about to walk away, the door opened and a workman came out. "Do you want to go inside and look around?" he asked. I was delighted. I walked down the stairs and found myself in a smallish room with low ceilings, red walls, and lots of tables. This was, I was informed, where all the Italians met in the sixties to hang out and socialize. I could easily imagine what it had been like, full of young people chatting, drinking, smoking.

I stayed there for a while and tried to imagine my birth father and birth mother meeting. I savored the moment. This was the closest I had ever been to my birth father, standing in a room in which he had also stood. Later, I walked up and down to all the Italian restaurants and barbers in the area with flyers and questions to see if anyone might have known this man, Vittorio, while my husband waited, patiently holding our son. But with no surname it was impossible. I knew it was a long shot, but as an adoptee, I couldn't just sit back and do nothing. I have to try and satisfy that part of myself.

After I found the restaurant where they had met, I walked the neighborhood with Pat, hoping it would jolt some further memory. But she stayed mainly silent except to reaffirm that she didn't know anything, she had no more memories. As we sat down to have lunch, I began to feel resigned that the effort had been useless. Just as we were leaving, though, she said, "Would you like to see the area where he worked?"

"Of course," I replied.

We walked through Soho, away from the club where they had met, into Piccadilly Circus where she pointed at a narrow street. "I think he worked down there," she said, "but I am not sure. It's the direction he went one evening. Would you like to see where we waited for a ride from our friends?"

We strolled to an area bustling with people and stood for a few moments in the spot they had stood. I imagined the two of them, how young they were, and I felt as though I had been given something of him.

More Searching

One Italian man responded to an advert I placed in an Italian newspaper. He was around the same age as my birth father, and he, too, used to hang out at Les Enfants. He told me that although he didn't remember ever knowing my birth father, he would be glad to meet up with me and give me suggestions. I was very nervous—after all, I had no idea who he was. We met in a restaurant, and I found myself studying his face, part of me hoping he really was Vittorio and was just checking me out. He told me a lot about the club and what it had been like in those days. I began to get more of a picture in my mind and it helped fill in a little piece. I was grateful for his kindness.

I also met with the local Italian priest, but to no avail and continued to go through my grief of not knowing. I still wish that Pat would willingly help me on my quest, but she won't. I have to bring up the subject or it is never spoken about. This has left me feeling betrayed. I really believed that Pat more than anyone would understand my need and do anything to help, but I was wrong. I didn't understand that she would have so many feelings about him and in other ways no feelings at all. From her perspective, she was the only parent who was important. She couldn't accept my need to know and I couldn't understand her attitude about it. This has caused great rifts in our relationship and made me feel distant from her and unable to trust her.

My baby has enormous blue eyes that could only be from my side. According to my [birth] information, my birth father had blue eyes, so I assume that's where they're from. They are her most remarkable feature and the most talked about and commented upon. It's a constant reminder of the unknown.

—Xaviera

Recently, I asked her again (this time, without any anger) and told her the truth: that I had been having a difficult time not knowing, that sometimes I look at my children and think it doesn't matter. At other times it matters so much that I can hardly bear it. I felt her listen and she has promised me that she will look into some things and see if she can help. I sensed a shift in her attitude.

Another Mystery

There is, however, yet another mystery surrounding my birthfather. Patricia met her husband, Franco, when she was twenty-one years old. Her parents were not happy as he also was Italian and he wasn't welcomed into the family at first. It wasn't until her parents understood that they were serious about getting married that they accepted him.

Pat and Franco moved into a large house split into bedsits, where many other couples lived. Pat didn't know any of her neighbors very well. Around the time of Roberta's birth, an Italian couple told Franco that they knew Pat had had a baby a few years earlier and had given it away. Pat had told Franco about me before they were married. It had been around my birthday and he had found her crying. She said she had to tell him the truth, that she couldn't marry him keeping such a secret.

When I met Franco, he said that he, too, had thought about me all these years and that he thought of me as a daughter. He was always very kind; once he looked at my hands and said, "You have Italian hands!" Pat was extremely surprised that these people knew about her earlier pregnancy, since she had told only one friend. She tells me news travels in the Italian community, and we have wondered for years how that couple knew. Perhaps they had been friends of my father.

I think about my birth father often, and irrational as it sounds, I still look for him on the street, sometimes catching the eye of a man about his age and imagining that is what he looks like.

I will never stop looking—I can't. It's an automatic reflex, and whether I will ever know him is a mystery. Sometimes I wonder if the universe is protecting me, if knowing him would cause only more pain. I don't have the illusion that he could fix me, but it would feel exhilarating to see his face.

The Impact of Adoption

I am so glad that my husband has been willing to learn more about adoption by attending conferences and discussions on adoption. It has strengthened our relationship and allowed me to open and trust him in a way that I never have before. As for Jonathan, he has gained a greater understanding of the impact of adoption on him and on our children.

That adoption was his problem too, dawned on him when I would tell him to leave over a minor argument, because "I know you'll leave eventually, so why waste time? Just go now!" He was slightly bewildered at first, but soon caught on that I didn't really mean it. Then he would reassure me that he wasn't going anywhere. I don't know how he could have been so patient, but he was. He explains to me now that all he saw was my pain and that he never took my rebukes personally. There are not many people in this world like my husband. (I, for one, take *everything* personally.)

Home is supremely important to me—as it always has been. I am not someone who never unpacks. I need my belongings around me for comfort and security. I have been able for the first time within a meaningful relationship to let the walls down, to let my husband see who the real Zara is. It is truly terrifying even today to show that side to another human being, but— thank goodness—harder still to keep all that inside. When you live with another person, he tends to notice (if he's not on drugs, that is) when you feel sad or mad.

In the past, however, I dealt with my emotions very differently, especially with boyfriends. When I began to search for my birth mother, for example, I was dating an actor. This seemed fun at the time. While seeing him, I had my meeting with the social worker, found out my birth mother's name, and sent off for my birth records. I had said not one word to him. One day he came over to see me, and I was being my usual aloof self, which translated as "I am so freaked out and feel like crying. Best not to show it."

I casually mentioned that maybe he had noticed I had been a little distant recently, to which he replied, "Yes, you're always a little distant." I asked him if he wanted to know why. "Okay," he replied calmly.

I loved drama, so I took a deep breath. "I just found out who my birth mother is. I know her name."

His mouth fell open. "You have been doing this and you *never* told me?" He was truly shocked. "Well, duh," he said, "no wonder you have been a little distant."

I looked at him and replied with a small smile, "Or maybe I'm just as good an actor as you."

Cellular Memory

I had never heard the term *cellular memory* before I attended adoption workshops, but now realize it is something I have experienced all my life. There are books for those who want to examine the subject in depth (see the Suggested Reading List at the back of this book), but for now, I will explain the concept as briefly and simply as I can.

It is believed that as the cells are being knitted together to form a new human life, before there are language and words, memories are formed of the time *in utero*. Whether it was a good experience or a bad one, whether the mother was overjoyed or contemplating abortion, the baby picks up those feelings. They remain with us inside our bodies in the form of physical memory. It is becoming common knowledge that babies in the womb respond to music, light, and sound, so it makes sense that a baby would also respond to its mother's stresses and joys.

For most of us, these memories are very deeply suppressed and the emotions surface only when the individual is exposed to situations that trigger them, such as the severing of important relationships. For many adoptees, getting married and having babies jump-starts the feelings. Questions start to formulate and the body remembers.

I felt a great sense of relief when this was finally explained to me. All my life, I had felt as if I was battling to prevent a force within me from surfacing, something so dreadful that it would surely devour me. In certain situations—sometimes just hearing a baby cry—I would slide into a pit of black despair that I didn't understand. As a child, I loved movies about animals, yet if there was a death or separation involved, I would have to leave the room. My parents would find me sobbing, sometimes uncontrollably, and the depression and sadness would swallow me again.

Even as an adult, I sometimes find myself thrown into total despair, unable to control myself or understand where my overwhelming sadness comes from. There are times when it is extremely embarrassing. Once I was at a wedding, a joyful occasion to which I had been looking forward. I had just split up with a lover—a man who really wasn't a suitable prospect for anything, the usual longhaired aging hippie drug-addict type that I found so attractive in those days. I had also started seeking help for my own little vices. Maybe it was a combination of all those things that led me to sitting alone at my allocated table, watching in the dimmed colored lights as the bride and groom began to dance. Other couples slowly joined them on the dance floor. What struck me the most was how happy and intimate the newlyweds looked. To my utter horror, I found myself crying. I knew I was in trouble—these tears weren't going to give up easily, and found myself weeping for all to see. My mother came over with a relative and they tried to comfort me and talk to me, but I just couldn't stop crying. The relative, a kindly, bosomy Jewish woman, sat and held my hand. She told me she was giving me healing, and I thought, "Hell, why not?" I let her hold my hand while I cried and the bride and groom, oblivious to everything but one another, carried on dancing around us.

Even after years in recovery, I still experienced tremendous discomfort in certain situations. For example, if I read or saw anything about babies or children being lost or taken from their parents, I became nauseous or felt an energy that filled my stomach and made breathing difficult. The fear that these sensations would envelope me caused me to find ways to turn them off: I avoided the subject or busied myself with something else so I wouldn't have to see what lurked underneath those feelings. I believed they were somehow part of who I was. Yet when Jonathan and I became engaged, the "body reactions," as I called them, became so powerful I knew I had to investigate further.

When the student is ready, says the old adage, the teacher appears. The same week that I told my husband I thought I needed help on my adoption issues (a hard thing for me to admit), a girl I barely knew—the neighbor of a friend of mine— introduced herself to me and said, "Oh, you may be interested in this book as you are new in LA." It was a directory for women, listing everything you could think of, from women-only fitness centers to good hairdressers. As I flipped through the pages, I saw a list of adoption-related agencies and services, including one therapist who specialized in adoption issues. I couldn't believe my eyes. I decided to phone, not knowing whether this therapist was considered competent or who she was.

I couldn't have been luckier. It turned out she was one of the best-known therapists in the LA adoption community and was an adoptee herself. She had a lot of experience in all matters involving adoption. I called her up to book an appointment and to find out more about her. She asked me a critical question. "What do you hope to gain from therapy? What are you looking for?"

I was completely stumped. "Hmmmm, I don't know," I replied uncertainly.

Nevertheless, she accepted me as her client. Just a few months later, I got pregnant with my son, and the body reactions became especially intense. When I told her about them, she explained the concept of cellular memory quite simply, in a way I could understand. "Your body remembers the time before you had language."

The relief I felt is difficult to describe. Her explanation made so much sense to me. I had been carrying these memories in my body my whole life. My body was trying to communicate with me, but I didn't know how to listen. I flashed back to a time in early recovery when a friend suggested that I go and see this amazing woman who did healing work. This healer had previously met my mother and knew some of my background. She had heard only recently that my brother was in treatment for heroin addiction and that it had been a very difficult time for me.

I didn't like that she knew so much about me and was willing to tell me what she knew. It made me very uncomfortable. She laid me on a table and started to place her hands on different parts of my body. I began to feel that familiar energy, the one that I always experienced when I saw anything about babies or loss. It was so overpowering that I jumped off the table and told her to stop, that it was too much. She dismissed my concern and told me that I had to go through it. We tried again. This time I hummed inside my head and thought about anything other than what was happening. Once again, I jumped off the table.

The healer became annoyed with me. She said she knew I had to deal with a lot because she had heard about my situation, but I had to stop jumping off the table. She was quite harsh. I went to see her a few more times, believing that she was correct and that I didn't have the right to demand respect for my feelings. I did not feel at all safe with her, yet because of my problems with self-esteem, I couldn't leave. Each appointment was hellish until finally I told a recovering friend. He said, "What are you doing? Don't go back!" I was so relieved to have permission to stop.

I wasn't able to continue any more bodywork until recently. I needed the knowledge gleaned from years of therapy to prepare me. I also needed people I could really trust and a supportive environment.

CHAPTER TWELVE

Miscarriage

In September, my friend had her second baby. Mine would have been due the following week. I spent two days crying before the grief finally began to lift.

I had had a miscarriage in March. I was ten weeks pregnant. At a routine checkup, my doctor could detect no heartbeat. In a way, I wasn't surprised—I hadn't felt a connection with the baby. At the time I got pregnant, I was scared to have another child. In retrospect, I realize that although I wanted more children, I was still resolving a lot of issues and needed more time. Yet everyone kept asking, and I had felt pressured somehow into creating the perfect family with the perfect age difference.

One morning a couple of weeks before the miscarriage, as I drove home from dropping Zachary at school, I suddenly felt an extremely powerful presence all around me, an energy that seemed to circle my head. I was certain that it was my baby. I began to weep as I drove, saying, "I don't want you to go, but if you have to, I won't try to stop you." Although I cannot explain how, I knew with unalterable certainty that its little soul had chosen to leave. I cried and cried.

I told no one, not even Jonathan. I thought he would chalk it up to me being a worrier. I went straight into denial and carried on as if I were still pregnant. Yet I began to feel too good, too normal again—my body stopped changing.

Later, I had the fateful ultrasound. Even though somewhere inside I had known all along, my conscious mind did not want to take it in. I stared blankly at my doctor, asking, "What do you mean, there is no baby? Are you sure?"

She looked me directly in the eye and repeated, "There is no baby. I am sorry. It just didn't develop properly."

I left her office sobbing and called Jonathan from the freeway. He left work and met me at the house. The feeling of emptiness enveloped me—it was so strange. One minute you're pregnant and the next, you're not. I couldn't get my mind around it at first. It was the same feeling as when someone dies. The emotional pain was extremely intense. I would try to rationalize that the baby wasn't really a baby. After all, I had been only ten weeks pregnant. Yet I knew that clump of tissue in my uterus had been a baby, regardless of my rationalizations

Next came the guilt—the baby had left me because I was so conflicted and it must have been confused by my emotions. I had an image of it saying, "I am not hanging around here with this crazy mother! I'm off to find one with more emotional balance." I also felt guilty that my body was defective somehow. Maybe I had eaten something bad for me; perhaps I hadn't taken good enough care of myself.

I really hoped that I would just get over it. After all, miscarriages happen all the time. Yet I was amazed at all the women who, when hearing about my miscarriage, came forward to reveal their own. I began to see that miscarriage was almost as much a secret as abortion. Women hid their grief, yet most of them never forgot their feelings and still thought of those pregnancies.

Although we never spoke of it, my mother had had miscarriages. I knew those miscarriages were the reason my brother and I had come into our parents' lives. Now I thought of my mother with a new a sense of compassion, not only for her but for all infertile women. How devastating to go through all the work of taking temperatures, having examinations, only to learn that your body, for whatever reason, is unable to carry a child to term. I reminded myself of how blessed I already was to have our son.

Many women who'd told me about their own miscarriages

said that they had got pregnant again very quickly. I hoped for that too—I wanted that awful pain of emptiness to disappear—but deep down I knew I wasn't ready. I couldn't force myself to heal. I had to go through the process of grief and mourning and learn their painful lessons.

My adoptive mother was infertile; she and my adoptive father tried for ten years before adopting. I grew up knowing how emotionally devastating infertility can be. Of course, there's a difference between intellectual knowledge and empathy. I couldn't really empathize until years later.
—Yvette

My miscarriage triggered my deep feelings around loss and shattered the fragile trust that I had begun to feel toward God or a higher power. He had pulled the rug out from under my feet, and I couldn't believe it had happened to me. I began to doubt my relationship with Him. I had to confront the harsh truth that I didn't trust nearly as much as I had hoped. All that work and my faith went straight out the window as soon as I lost the new baby. Worse, I felt incredible fear: what else was going to happen? What else would He take away from me? I began to slide down that dark slope into depression.

It was during that bleak period that I came closest to using drugs again. I actually thought about it, yet somehow managed to hang on. I realized that I had to rebuild my foundation. I had a choice about how to see my life: I could look only at the negative or I could emphasize the positive. It took all the energy I could muster to accept that my miscarriage had happened for a reason. It caused me to question my faith, something that would ultimately deepen and strengthen my spiritual development. I also had to accept that I do not recover from emotional injuries quickly. I have to work through my feelings bit by bit, no shortcuts. If I had gotten pregnant again quickly, I would have bypassed the work that now gives my life direction.

Healing and Writing

A few months after my miscarriage, Jonathan and I went out to dinner. I said, "I feel like I am just sitting around waiting to get pregnant, counting the days, disappointed each month. It's no good for me. I need to write about my experiences as an adoptee having my own child. It's time to write down all those feelings I had with Zachary, and I want to find out if other mothers who were adopted feel like me."

Jonathan listened patiently, and the more I talked, the more I began to feel really excited at the prospect of compiling a book. I suddenly recognized that I had a purpose, that all the pain had been worth it, that having been adopted was worth it if I could tell my story and help others.

Later, I buried the baby book I had started under a new tree that Zachary and I planted together. It was my way of recognizing the miscarriage and the life that had briefly resided within me. After we had finished the planting, I sat back on my heels quietly looking at the tree. Zach, too, sat quietly next to me. He put his hand on my knee and said, "Don't worry. Mummy, she will come back again."

I still think of that lost baby and work out how old it would be now if it had stayed. But I also believe that if it hadn't left me, I would never have developed the qualities and strengths that shape my life today.

Birth terrified me—every aspect, physically and emotionally. I doubt I would ever have had children had I not been married to a man who wanted them very much. I had the not-uncommon adoptee's feeling that I had never been born, so how could I give birth?
—Zoe

Six months later I was pregnant with my first daughter, quickly followed by our second. Did "she," as Zachary predicted, come back again after all?

Guy Fawkes Day 1999

I was pregnant again. Could it be true? I wanted to doubt, so I did two tests just to make sure. Nevertheless, there it was in front of me, those two red lines. *Wow!* I was filled with delight—then fear. What if I had another miscarriage? I couldn't cope. What if I carried another child to term? What if it was a girl?

That overwhelmed me—a girl, a daughter, a mother-daughter relationship. I was afraid, yet so excited. And that day was my birthday, a day I never looked forward to. A day that had always been filled with difficult emotions could be different now. My emotions were all over the place. What a gift—my birthday would never be the same again! I felt it was another sign from the Universe: let go, Zara, of your image of being a mistake. You are going to bring another child into this world.

My feelings of fear around having a girl stemmed from the fact that my adoptive mother and I had never really gotten along. We both tried so hard, and there is no denying the love between us. Yet we have always been mismatched. Our opinions, our interests, our taste in clothes, books, are as different as they can be. Many people who aren't adopted tell me they feel different from their mothers, too, but genetics play a big part. The longer I am a mother, the more I realize this.

The sadness I experience today about our inability to connect leaves me feeling somewhat motherless. Yet she has done so much for me: as a child, she bought me clothes whenever I needed them; she came to all my school plays. But I have always felt like the wrong daughter for her, that if she had been able to have her own daughter, they would have been so much closer and connected on an emotional level. I have often found myself thinking about that daughter, and sometimes I almost feel her presence.

I felt myself beginning to change: I had to remember I deserve wonderful things. I had a right, just like other women, to have more children. It was a whole new mindset. The strangest part was I had never realized when I was younger that the notion

I was a mistake, because I was adopted, was the basis of what I really believed about myself.

Superman

My son decided he wanted to watch the men who were assembling some furniture we had just bought for the baby. I was hugely pregnant, only a few more weeks to go, and puttering around the house. I could hear Zachary from the other room chatting away to the workmen. He is a very friendly boy and never has trouble talking to people—so different from how I was as a child! I never enjoyed speaking to grownups, especially people I didn't know.

My son brought in his toolbox to show the workmen what he had and then I heard him say proudly, "My mum is just like Superman!" I stopped in my tracks; there was no answer from the men.

"My mum is just like Superman!" he exclaimed again.

I am? I thought, slightly confused. I waited to listen where my son couldn't see me.

"She's adopted, just like Superman."

"Oh," I heard a man reply.

When I entered the room, I almost felt embarrassed that he had revealed my adoption to these strangers. Yet I was flattered that my son connected me to his favorite superhero.

My Daughter

One night I had a powerful dream. I was offering to help a man find his birth daughter, and my mum asked if I could help find a baby for her friends to adopt. I started screaming that I didn't believe in adoption, that a baby should stay with its mother and not be taken away. In a rage, I screamed over and over that adoption was wrong, and that if it really was necessary for the child to be taken away from its mother, the birth mother should be in touch regularly and be able to see her child. I gave birth the day after that dream.

The birth was much easier in many ways than my son's birth had been. Although the labor was intense, we played music and I sang and wept and said I couldn't do it, it was too hard. Suddenly, at one point during transition and deep pain, I had this overwhelming certainty that the baby was a girl. As I sang along to the music, I felt such energy. It was so powerful. I began to cry with joy and pain. Her birth was so beautiful and she was so wanted! I wept for myself and for Pat, my birth mother. How different it had been for us!

I felt immediate connection with both my babies. When I was in transition and most women are screaming and yelling and asking for pain medication, I was laughing and joking. All through transition and delivery I was just so happy to have my babies, I couldn't understand how women could complain. It was the best!

— Ashley

I pushed the baby out in fifteen minutes. "It's a girl, it's a girl," I said over and over. "I have a boy and now I have a girl! How come I get to be so lucky?" The nurses and doctor laughed, and as a lullaby played in the background, I held my tiny, perfect daughter and felt instant love. How could I have doubted that I wouldn't have enough love for more than one child? As my OB cleaned us up, she also sang along to the lullaby and the atmosphere was tranquil and spiritual. There was a reverence, a sacred quality that is difficult to describe. It was a wonderful birth, just what I had hoped for. We named her Kayla Rae.

I truly enjoyed being a new mother again. It was not as intense as with Zachary, but I had moments when I looked at Kayla and wondered how anyone could give up her baby. How could you do that, and if you do, how do you keep from going insane? Just the thought of Kayla being taken from me made me feel insane. These visions of her being stolen were just like the ones I had seen with Zachary, but this time I refused to let them take control. I shouted, "Go away! You are not going to spoil this time for me. We are safe. My baby is safe and I am allowed to be happy. I am allowed to have two children, just like other people." Each night as we drifted off to sleep next to each other, I stared at her and cried a little with sheer gratitude and wonder. I thanked God from the deepest place in my heart for giving me these children.

My pregnancy was filed with excitement and longing to see my baby, to hold him and play with him and watch him grow up. I can only wonder what it was like for my birth mother since I know she made a plan to give me up for adoption early in her pregnancy. I cannot imagine having done it myself.
—Bethany

Someone Who Looks Like Me

People say my daughter looks just like me, but I cannot really believe I was ever that pretty as a baby or as cute as she is. Some days I look at her and wonder who her mother is. Then I realize it's me, and I am totally in love again; I feel connected and know she is part of me. Often I find myself looking at a huge photograph of my daughter. It is so familiar to me, yet it also feels odd. It takes me a moment to realize why—I am looking at someone who looks like me.

I love watching my children together; I can see their connection. I love the way Kayla smiles at Zachary, and I am fascinated by their similarity. So this is what it's like to look like your sibling! I wonder whether I will always feel that way, that for me it will always feel somewhat strange to now be in a blood-related family.

It's remarkable how my daughter and I look alike. It gives me a warm, wonderful feeling.
—Cybil

Birthday Blues

Recently, I have begun to realize how important a birth story is to a child. My son loves to hear about his birth, what he looked like, where was he before he was with me. His questions have allowed me to experience the depth of my feelings around this issue about which I had tremendous sadness.

> *My second daughter and I looked so much alike as babies, I almost felt like I had been replaced. It was really odd to have someone look like me. I was so bonded to my daughter for that, it almost scared me.*
> *—Tanya*

I remember lying with Jonathan one day and thinking about the fact that my own birth had been so different and how sad I felt about that—and probably always had. There had been no flowers, no visitors, no phone calls, no celebration—just a terrified young mother left to go through labor alone, knowing she would be giving up her child.

My adoptive parents certainly celebrated my arrival at their home, but I was two months old. I had already had two mothers— my birth mother and a foster mother—and now my adoptive mother. I truly believe that even if a child is adopted on the day of its birth, the sense of abandonment will be the same and the grief will go unresolved. In recent years, some close friends of mine have suffered the deaths of people they love, and I have watched them struggle with

> *My birthday is so horrendous, but for my daughter I have to make it perfect—a huge celebration.*
> *—Delle*

their grief. The anniversary of a death is a particularly difficult time. For adoptees, birthdays are an anniversary too—the anniversary of their separation and abandonment, the day their mothers gave them away. However, this phenomenon goes unacknowledged in our society.

The two weeks or so both before and after my birthday have always been hard for me. A baby picks up on its mother's anxiety and disconnection *in utero*. The baby knows that it is going to be given away, and experiences panic and fear for its survival because it knows it needs its mother to keep it alive. On the day of birth, a baby may or may not see its mother. One thing both mother and baby know is that they will be separated.

I remember walking through the store on my birthday to get plates and cups and feeling this cold air on me. It is a really powerful sensory memory. When I explained it to my therapist, it was like a rebirthing, like I was coming out to the world and I was alone. Every birthday I experience that feeling of my birth mother saying "no," and there being no other mother yet. I feel like I am going to disappear down a huge dark hole. When I am trying to separate from my adoptive parents, it's the same feeling.
—Erika

I have known adoptees who have such severe depression around their birthdays that they are literally incapable of doing anything constructive. I have seen them walk into adoption-support meetings and share what they are feeling and for others to express that they, too, have the same experience. Their relief and surprise are genuine. It's comforting to know that I'm not alone, that other adoptees have this experience, too.

As I approach my thirty-ninth birthday, I am able to observe myself a little more. I am able to catch myself in the process that I go through. It is very important that my birthday be acknowledged, yet I also want the day to be over. Even though I have been in reunion a long time, there is still a physical reaction of despair and sadness. I find myself, without wanting to, to feeling what I can now put into words—the separation from my mother. And these days, I think of my birth father, too. Growing up, I was so preoccupied by thoughts of my mother that I never thought about my father. But today I am much more aware of how I miss him. I feel the loss of not knowing, much like I did before I met Pat. I feel the loss of siblings, grandparents, aunts, uncles, and cousins, and I am sometimes jealous of others who have spent time with their fathers. I know that my father's family is out there somewhere and I don't know where.

Perhaps I will never know my birth father—with each year that passes, finding a man whose first name is all I know becomes less and less likely. I still have days when I find myself sinking and feeling hopeless and being so angry at my powerlessness. I have struggled with thoughts of my conception and wondered about the loveless merging of two strangers that created me. I must believe it was God's work, that for whatever reason, I chose this path. This is what keeps me from sinking into self-pity, unable to be productive. I have to acknowledge the feelings and move on.

Yesterday, an adoptee told me it was her daughter's first birthday. A lot of feelings were coming up for her—despair and panic at how she would get through the day emotionally. It reminded me of Zachary's first birthday and how I felt. I didn't realize what was going on. All I knew was I had to keep busy so I wouldn't feel. *Feel what?* Like I did at my own day of birth? Yet this day was different, it was a celebration of my child. How I wanted it to be perfect! Yes, I went over the top. I bought too many gifts, asked too many people, but I wanted everyone to know what a special day it was and for Zachary to be the center of attention. I wanted him to know that we remembered his birthday, that it was special. When it came time to cut the cake, I was a mess. How would I contain myself? When everyone sang to him, I barely managed, but I still wonder at the magnitude of those emotions. Why did I want to curl up and howl?

As a child, I knew that I was supposed to enjoy and be happy on my birthday, so I never let on the depression I felt. I thought that there was something desperately wrong with me. I remember one birthday when all the children were having a great time watching the holiday fireworks out the long window overlooking the garden. Everyone made the right fireworks-appreciation sounds, but I felt such despair that I crept off to be alone. After a time I was able to join the party again. I was seven years old.

My birthday was always the time when I wondered about my birth mother. As a small child, I would look up at the big sky and wonder if she were standing under it, too. Did she think of me on this day? Sometimes I could almost feel her, yet I worried that I had been forgotten. I carried that fear throughout life: Have I been forgotten? Do people remember me when I am not in sight? As a child, what was particularly hard was my inability to express myself. My mother had no inkling of what was going on inside me; I always hoped she would somehow be able to guess.

My first birthday celebration with my birth family was scary. I didn't want to go, but it seemed very important to Pat. I brought my girlfriend Virginia along to the restaurant for support. I was bombarded with presents. I think Pat wanted to make up for all those years she hadn't been able to give me something, and it was bittersweet. Guilt began to come back big and strong. How could I accept these presents? Did I have a right to them? How would my adoptive family feel if they knew what I was doing?

I could feel Pat's emotion. There was so much to say, yet nobody did. Instead, we carried on in our awkwardness to do what one was supposed to do on birthdays. All those years apart, and here we were together, celebrating. It felt so strange.

CHAPTER THIRTEEN

Telling Our Children

I had often wondered how I would explain being adopted to Zachary, who at the time was just under three-and-a-half years old. I still had the tendency to protect both families, but I didn't want to lie to him or keep secrets. Yet at times it was easier to just not mention certain things, to not include certain people, especially when I still had my own issues to work through. Why was I still hiding?

I was with Zachary one day as he sat on the toilet, and we were talking about our visit to London earlier that year, specifically the visit to Pat. I said, "You know, Zachary, she is your grandma, too, like Grandma Jean," (my mother).

He listened as I told him I had been given to Grandma Jean because Grandma Pat couldn't take care of me. Zachary wanted

I told my children as soon as they could understand what it meant that I was adopted. They knew I didn't grow up knowing I was adopted, and they were very interested when I completed my search. Their father and I used to tease them when they were teenagers about how baldness comes from the maternal line and we didn't know if my relatives were bald. When I found my birth mother, I was talking on the phone with her with the boys in the room. They heard me ask her if my brothers still have hair. I could see them both leaning in to hear what the answer was— both of my birth brothers are quite bald! They [my boys] are both very glad I found my birth mother for my sake as well as theirs.

—Frieda

149

to know why Grandma Pat couldn't take care of me. I didn't know what to say, so I told him that it was because she was young and it was too hard for her. All the reasons I gave sounded strange even to me, not good enough reasons to be given way.

My son thought for a while and then asked, "Was there a cord?" I hesitated, unsure of what he meant. He asked again, "Was there a cord?

I finally understood. "Between Grandma Jean and me?"

"Yes," he said.

I shook my head. "No, there wasn't." With that, he hopped off the toilet and went on to something else. I stood rooted to the floor for a moment, amazed. At only three-and-a-half, Zachary really had got it!

Telling the Truth

As my children grow older, I find myself now faced with a new challenge: honesty. I see already that I don't always want to include Pat as "Grandma Pat" in conversation with them for fear that they will say something to my parents. I know my mum and dad would find it hard if they knew the children also called Pat their grandmother. So here I am, repeating some of my old behavior, living in the silence I grew up with.

I realize yet again that I have to stop protecting everyone else's feelings, that they have a right to feel whatever they feel, and that it is my children's birthright (like it is mine) to know their genetic heritage. Some days I am angry when Pat sends a card to one of the children and signs it "Grandma." I think, *What right does she have to that title? She lost that privilege!* But at the same time, I want my children to feel free to ask questions about adoption, about both their families, without my unresolved baggage clouding their lives. They have a right to relationships with all members of my birth family and my adoptive family as well.

They are still young, so who knows what they will experience as time passes. But I would be in denial to say that adoption is not also a major part of their lives, too, obviously not as much as it has been in mine. Still, I do not want my children to have to keep quiet the way I did through fear of others' reactions and possible rejection.

My boys have known I was adopted from day one. They do wish they had a complete family history now that they have children.
—Glynis

I feel that not telling my daughters I am adopted is the same as not telling an adoptee they are adopted; it is who they are, it is their heritage.
—Hazel

I strive to accomplish a home where it is safe for them to speak out and to have relationships without my feeling threatened. I realize the only way to accomplish this is to continually work on my issues, my prejudices, and not to use my children as pawns in any way.

Letting Go of Grief

In the early years of my recovery, attending meetings, my skin crawled as I heard people talk about their "inner child." I thought they were pathetic, that they used this inner-child idea as an excuse to act childishly and not take responsibility for the fact they were now grownups. My friends and I would laugh at their expense. Yet why, when I sat in those meetings and heard the sharing, was I not only embarrassed at their honesty but also uncomfortable and so deeply sad?

I had spent most of my life to that point unwilling and unable to show anybody my pain. I was never able to sit still for a moment—I rushed about smoking cigarettes, taking drugs, and talking on the phone. When I felt that familiar pang deep in my stomach, I knew what to do: call a friend, anything but wait to see what came up.

In my early recovery, I was cynical of everyone. I still

couldn't show much vulnerability, and there were many ways to stop feeling aside from drugs: compulsive talking, reading *Hello* magazine, obsessing about someone else's life, or just busying myself with tasks. Sitting still can be a struggle even today, yet when I allow myself the time to sit quietly, it is always beneficial. Sadness passes a lot quicker if I simply allow myself to cry. The most liberating part is the softness of heart that comes with it, the insight and ability to see others' pain and joy, to break out of my isolation and rejoin the human race. Until I had experienced my grief, I was incapable of experiencing joy. The two are intertwined. We cannot have one without the other.

Today I am happy to say that I experience much joy in my life. When I don't, it is because I am afraid to allow it in for fear of loss. To fully love another human being is indeed fraught with risk, yet if I had chosen not to face myself, I would have missed out on the greatest gift in life.

When a person goes through a severe trauma—the sudden death of a loved one, rape, an automobile accident—their world is rocked to the very core. They can feel like they have lost their foundation, and their trust in life may disappear as they grasp to find new meaning. The good news is that friends, family, and professional counselors recognize the trauma and acknowledge their pain. Eventually, these people can look back and remember a time when life was good. This can give them hope that, although their lives have changed, they can find security and happiness again.

For adoptees, there is no life before the trauma. Often the trauma takes place *in utero*, so there is no memory of feeling whole and secure. Their lives start with unrecognized trauma. When the adopted baby is brought home by his new parents there is, of course, much celebration. But while Mom and Dad are showing off their new baby to relatives and friends, laughing and talking with all the joy they feel, the baby is quietly wondering, "Who are these people? This woman doesn't smell like my mother. Where did my mummy go?" The baby grows up with his loss unrecognized and unresolved. Yet at some point, the body can contain the emotions no more. They have to be expressed and will find a way to come out, often in destructive ways.

I recently attended an adoption workshop. The facilitator asked us to look at slides of pregnant woman and women giving birth. We were not to look at the woman, but to focus only on the baby, to think of our own births and wonder who we looked at, who held us. For me, it was nearly unbearable, because I couldn't help but see myself as those newborns.

Tears started and I tried not to focus on the baby but rather the whole picture. I began to have feelings of not being welcomed. It was not a place I wanted to go. I thought of my own babies, the joy, the excitement, the thrill of seeing them for the first time. I remembered how I held them and studied them and talked to them, how wanted and loved they were. I burst into tears, my body reacting violently to each image of these babies.

I realized that the feeling I experienced as I viewed those images was not only very familiar, but that I still carried it around within me. All the years of drug taking, shouting at my mother, running off and partying, and still today of separating myself from my husband and my children when it gets too hard, were to protect myself from the grief of that loss because it feels like it will kill me. I carry it even today; it still comes up when I least expect it, just when I think I've finally been able to let it go. I am saddened that after all this time it is still with me. Nonetheless, it is helpful to finally understand what it is and that it does eventually pass.

I am a mother of three incredible children. I am married to a warm and caring husband. Yet in a flash I can feel separate even from them, from my own blood. I fear they will reject me, that I am not a good-enough mother, that they can see there is a part of me that still believes I am worthless, unwanted, and that my family and my friends know I was not meant to be here. I am learning to accept that this memory will continue to come up from time to time. I also know it is possible, with help, to release it and not be a victim to it.

It is essential that the adopted child's grief is recognized so that he or she can then connect with other people. Until I could recognize my loss and allow my grief to surface, I was incapable of developing a trusting relationship or having a healthy marriage.

Religion

I have begun to attend synagogue, not really through any great calling, but basically because in LA, most of the pre-schools are attached to religious institutions. Even though I have not participated in my faith in recent years, I felt more comfortable sending Zachary to a school whose sponsor was at least familiar to me. I watch my son enjoy the concepts of God and all the stories and traditions of Judaism. He is proud to be Jewish. He talks about it often and he asks many questions about God and life. And because I want him to have some answers, I now find myself reading up on holidays and stories. It is a commitment to send one's child to a school of faith. It takes effort and it also pushes me to look at my prejudices and my beliefs. How much easier it would be to just send him to a school with no denomination!

Recently, during a group discussion, our rabbi asked us to think about how we felt about being Jews. He asked us to reach back into childhood for memories of faith and tradition, so we could bring them to consciousness when we needed them. He told the story of an old woman who lived in a convalescent home. Every Friday night, she imagined herself lighting the Shabbat candles and saying the prayers, even though she was just sitting in her chair. It brought her great comfort.

As the rabbi continued, I began to feel a deep pain in my heart. I had flashes of our family sitting around the table at Passover, reading prayers and eating. I remembered going to synagogue as a child, and I saw the faces of people I hadn't thought about in many years. But what was most distinct was the emptiness I felt, the lack of connection. There was no comfort to grasp onto. As a teenager, I watched the other Jewish girls, and yet I didn't feel like them. I felt my body type was different and sometimes they would say, "You don't look Jewish."

The others in the group saw my tears and asked me to share. I found myself saying for the first time that I had never felt Jewish, that I had never been able to embrace Judaism because, as an adoptee, I was never sure if that's really who I was. Mum had always assured me that my birth mother had been Jewish, but for some reason I never believed her. So even though I wanted so badly to feel a part of Judaism, I felt only emptiness, misplacement. I cannot emphasize what a revelation this was for me. Up until that point, I had never realized that my adoption had kept me apart from not only my family, but from God as well.

Even though it has felt extremely liberating for me to finally make that connection, the truth is, I am half-Italian. There is a whole side to me that I don't know anything about. It is not enough to say I am a Jew because my mother is Jewish; it does not fulfill that yearning to know my Italian side. Today, I find myself watching my children with their father and thinking how they all fit together. It is still hard some days to feel I am part of this unit, too. Most people, whether they get along with their families or not, don't even think about a sense of connection. They share the same bloodline, the same heritage; it is a spiritual connection.

I am not saying there is no spiritual connection with my adoptive family, only that as a child I didn't feel it. Paradoxically, since I have been reunited with my birth family—and especially since I've become a mother—I am more able to experience the spiritual connection with my adoptive family and feel more a part of them. But I had to heal my wound before I could experience that connection. Today, I believe I was meant to be adopted. For reasons beyond my knowledge, this was my assigned path. It has made me who I am today.

Challenges

Parenting is indeed the hardest work I love to do. From everything I have read and from all the mothers I've spoken to, what I realize more and more is that it is up to me to not pass down my baggage to my children. Since I have carried both my adoptive and my birth mothers' feelings and fears, I am still challenged when it comes to separating what truly belongs to me. The commitment to bring emotionally healthy children into adulthood forces me to continue to work through my difficulties and take responsibility for my stuff.

I have already seen how my insecurity can affect my children: there are days when I don't know if my children love me and when I am scared that my daughters and I will go through the same painful clashes that my mother and I endured. Sometimes I catch myself projecting my unresolved conflicts onto my daughter. I have to keep being reminded—or reminding myself—that she is not me; she has her own feelings about life. I hope she will see situations in a very different way than I do. The main fact is that she is not adopted, so that makes us different from the beginning. She won't have to spend her childhood looking for her mother on every street, and I will not have to constantly be on the lookout for my child nor deal with the pain of infertility.

Last night I watched my husband with my daughter and delighted in their connection. She adores her daddy, and he of course is besotted with her. It reminds me of how I was with my son when he was first born, how special and all-enveloping it was and still is. As I watched her small body relax and heard her cooing as she gave in to sleep, I could sense her contentedness. I felt happy and then a sadness. I was never held by my birth father; he has never even seen me. We don't know each other at all, and even though I know my adoptive father loves me, I still feel that longing.

There are days when I am fatigued and need some alone time, and the last thing I want to do is be patient, tolerant, and loving. Sometimes I tell my children, "I am sorry, but I am not having a good day. It's not your fault." But the reality is that my kids cannot say, "See you, Mum! We're going out for awhile. We'll be back when you have calmed down." They are infants, stuck all day with me, so it is my responsibility, whether I feel like it or not, to make their day enjoyable and safe for them to be who they are.

Needing Help

I realize today that Pat and I needed both individual help and help together to process our relationship. If we had had that help right at the start, maybe we wouldn't have had such a difficult time the first few years. We will never really know.

For awhile I received many abusive letters from Pat. She was angry at me for being the way I was. She did not understand why I needed to know who my birth father was and told me that I never would find him. I wrote back as best I could, trying not to dump on her all the rage I felt. I tried to detach and understand that it wasn't about me, that I had become the target for all the pain and anger she felt toward her own family for the way they had handled her pregnancy.

It was truly the hardest time for me, and finally I broke off all communication, telling Pat I had to stop opening her letters, that they hurt too much, that I felt she needed help. I had to concentrate on my recovery, so it was still many years before I myself got the help I needed with professionals on adoption. Recovery programs saved my life, but the focus is on addiction,

My birth mother is willing to go only so far in her own healing. She is not willing to go back to when she had me, which puts a roadblock in our relationship. I seem to trigger her seventeen-year-old that gave birth to me, and she is full of shame when she goes back there. It's just explosive—it's the same explosive energy I had to work through in my therapy. But she doesn't have anybody to talk to.

—Iris

not adoption. What Pat and I both needed was someone to explain that we were triggering each other's initial loss and that we couldn't fix each other. We each had to deal with our losses separately.

My experience shows me there will always be a part of me that wants to run and hide and not feel when things get tough. It would be detrimental to think that the old Zara has completely gone away. There are times when life feels overwhelming, and I think about partying or using something to numb my feelings. Luckily, I now have healthier coping tools: I can call someone, sit with the emotions and know they will indeed pass. Today I have too much to lose to take risks with my addictions. I know I could be back there in a heartbeat. But the good news is that I have found I can go through extremely painful situations sober; I can survive them and come out the other side stronger and more whole than I was before.

Looking for my birth mother brought up so many buried emotions that some days it went beyond pain. The grief would take me over in such a way that I would spend hours staring at the walls, numb and broken. At the same time, I knew that drugs, alcohol, or sex would be only a temporary relief. There were moments when I thought I would never make it. Yet I did, sometimes minute by minute, calling friends when I was in extreme panic or just sitting paralyzed on the floor. As I experienced the very depth of my pain, I began to develop a relationship with myself in a way I never had before. I found strength from my higher power that continues to affirm I don't have to do this alone, that I cannot muster this strength on my own, that I need to go to that source.

Getting Help

To any adoptee searching for help and support, I say this: find people who *really* know and understand the adoption experience, and stay away from people who *think* they know. Avoid like the plague those who are just interested in being a part of your reunion stories because it sounds like fun. Be open to professional counseling to understand and help process all the conflicting emotions you may feel so your reunion can be the best possible experience; so that you, as an adoptee, can pass on to your children the joy in their arrival that was never felt at your own. (See the Resources Guide at the back of this book for further information on getting help.)

I also would like to add that having children can be extremely intense and can bring up a lot of suppressed emotions. I have been told it is extremely common for adoptees—both men and women—to want to search for their birth families after they themselves become parents. They may feel a lot of depression once the baby comes, or be taken back to their own experience *in utero* and during birth.

Becoming pregnant the first time brought my search to the forefront. It had always been something I would do someday until I got pregnant. It took me eight more years to complete, but I knew I would never give up until I found the answers to my questions for my children and myself.

—Jeanne

I am not against adoption. I do think, however, it should be done very differently. Records should not be closed as they still are in some parts of the United States. I do not believe it is better for adoptees to not see their birth mothers as they grow up. Contrary to popular wisdom, I do not believe this would make the adoptee confused or emotionally

When my son broke his neck and the surgeons came to me and asked those hated questions—"Is there any bone disease in your family?", etc.— I truly wanted to die. Here was a life-and-death situation and I had no answers. I will never forgive the government for not giving me this important life-saving information. (My son is perfectly fine now. We were lucky.)

—Kendall

unbalanced. In my experience, it is *not* knowing your birth parents that causes deep, long-term damage. It affected every single relationship I had and how I perceived (and still perceive myself) as a human being.

I saw an advertisement recently that said that children from single mothers who didn't know their fathers or weren't raised by their fathers were 80 percent more likely to use drugs than children raised by two parents. What many people don't know is that adoptees are the largest minority of people who are institutionalized or who suffer from various forms of addiction or mental-health problems.

Just because a child is given two parents and told to call them Mum and Dad, it doesn't mean he/she will escape feeling rejected by his/her birth mother. When I hear that so-and-so has adopted and how excited they are after waiting years for a baby, I always want to say, "Yes, it is tremendously exciting to have a child. I am sure you will be the best parents you can, but please don't forget who the baby is. Allow him to grieve the loss of his birth mother, respect his right to his heritage, and you will have an incredible relationship."

In situations where the mother really doesn't want contact or the child was abandoned, it is equally as important to acknowledge the loss and to respect the child's heritage and, if possible, have some relations with other blood relatives. Recently I was talking with some people about adoption. We had a heated debate: they said, "But adoption is good for the child! Where would some children be with out it? Your adoptive parents are your parents, aren't they? Does it matter where you came from?"

My reply was, as always, the same. "Yes, they are my parents, but unlike non-adoptees, I also have another set of parents. I know my adoptive parents love me and I love them, but I have a different connection with them than I would experience if I had been raised in my birth home. I still need to know who my birthparents are."

I am sorry my adoptive parents were not given the information that is available today when they adopted me. Maybe it would have made being parents easier for them and less painful when they learned of my brother's and my addictions; perhaps it would have eliminated some of the grief we put them through.

Since becoming a mother, I have been much more able to put myself in both my birth mother's and adoptive mother's situations. I have felt compassion for both. As for my adoptive mother, if I could not have had my own children, I do not know how I would have managed. Having children has meant everything to me; it has given me a sense of purpose and I feel connected to the human race.

As for my birth mother, she was only a baby herself. She had neither job skills nor resources nor real support. Even so, the baby in me will never understand why she didn't fight to keep me. Therefore, I am grateful for the stories other birth mothers have told me. They have helped me to understand that they are not merely women who just didn't care, or that giving up their babies meant nothing to them.

As for me, I hope the part of me that still believes there was something wrong with me will diminish with the passage of time.

Being a mother made me think much more often about being adopted. I had always accepted the fact that I was adopted. I was raised knowing that she (my birthmother) did the best thing for me at the time. But once my children were here, I kept finding myself wishing that I knew who she was and where she was, wondering if she was thinking about me. There were nights I would lie in bed and in my head I would scream out for her to contact me. The pain was horrible.
—Laurel

I don't resent her one bit. She could have had an abortion! I feel sorry for this woman who never knew what happened to her baby.
—Maria

My Brother's Search

I was lucky enough to meet Grant's full-blood sister on a visit to London in the summer of 1999. My brother always told me he had no interest in finding a mother who didn't want him, but at age thirty-six, he changed his mind. While he was in the process of his search, he began to call me on the phone for long talks. I felt honored that Grant would confide in me, and I was also interested in all the information he acquired. I felt like I was in it with him and I knew what he was going through. During those conversations, we began to talk in a way we never had before. I was able to share with him my feelings growing up as an adoptee, and it helped us heal our relationship. We both gained a much deeper understanding of each other.

Sadly, Grant's mother has not been ready to meet him (so far), and I imagine that is a terrible rejection for him. Nevertheless, his sister and he have developed a close, warm relationship. I felt quite nervous meeting her, and I have to admit that even though I was happy to hear about his reunion, I felt a slight pang of jealousy that they were such good friends. I wondered how I would fit into his life now that he had his birth sister. I also felt a little annoyed that she hadn't had to go through all the years of his childhood and his drug days and could enjoy him now as a grown man.

I opened the door to a woman who was indeed my brother's blood sister. I was fascinated. They had the same smile, they looked alike. Well, of course they *would* look alike, wouldn't they? They are full-blood siblings. But to me it was a surreal moment and one that I will always remember as the three of us—Grant and his two sisters—stood together. We sisters, both so much a part of him and his life, were strangers to one another. I sat them next to each other on the sofa and took photos. The whole time I was thinking, "They fit! They look alike!"

EPILOGUE

Sources of Strength

I cannot believe how much I have learned in the last few years. I owe my strength to my husband and our children. They are the catalyst that has propelled me to this new level of understanding. I gave birth to my third child while completing this book. I haven't added much about the pregnancy or birth for fear of repeating myself, but I will tell you that it was much easier in many ways than the first two. I did not regress as I had done in the past.

I was scared to have another daughter, and couldn't explain to myself exactly why, so I decided I must definitely be carrying a boy. Nevertheless, a week before giving birth, I dreamed the baby was a girl. It was suggested that the similarities I feel between myself and our first daughter, Kayla, were too much for me to take in. The sense of connection has almost been overwhelming.

> *I remember when they brought my daughter to me seven hours after the birth. I took one look at her and knew that she was mine.*
> *—Nadine*

I was able to deliver the new baby, Arden, totally naturally, without drugs. When they handed her to me I felt a microsecond of fear, of wanting to disconnect, but I spoke to her immediately to reassure her that this was my stuff. As I put her to my breast and enjoyed those sacred first few hours with my new daughter,

I was certain that we were meant to be together and that Kayla and she would be true sisters. That meant they would have something I didn't have, and it dawned on me that I had been afraid of that, too.

I had a sister, yet we hadn't grown up together. Like my birth mother, I had a son and two daughters, except I got to keep my two girls and Pat didn't. As I watch her grow, I find myself searching my littlest daughter's face. She has her own look, yet there is a difference between her and my other children. Does she resemble my birth father? I look for clues in her face and her hair and her body. It is my only way of imagining what he may look like. Recently, Zachary overheard me and Jonathan talking about my birth father. He began to question me: "What is a birth father?" And why didn't I find him?

I replied that I had tried, but it was too hard with so little information. Zachary persisted. "Why don't you try again?"

I sighed. "I don't really know what else to do, and it takes a lot of energy that I don't have right now."

"What is his name?" my son asked.

"Vittorio. That's all I know." I began to feel very strange discussing this with my son. Zachary kept his steady eye on me, and I looked away—I could feel the tears wanting to escape.

"Mummy," he said solemnly, "when I am older, I am going to help you find him."

The tears came and I hugged him tightly. "That is an incredibly kind thing for you to do for me," I told him.

My Life Today

Today, as I come to the end of this book, Zachary is seven years old, Kayla is three and Arden is a year old. My feelings surrounding adoption are still very much present, yet they do not overwhelm me as much as they did when I first had my son. Having children has brought back long-dormant childhood memories. For instance, I had an extreme fear that my parents would die and I would end up in a children's home. I would lie in bed at night and beg God not to take them from me. I also had nightmares about them dying and would sometimes go to their bedroom in the middle of the night to reassure myself that they were still breathing. I resumed these night checks with my own babies and continue them even now from time to time.

I continue to suffer separation anxiety—maybe all that is just part of what it is to be a mother. But I still cannot let even my husband take Arden for a walk without feeling uncomfortable, so I tell him. Jonathan respects that part of me and doesn't push to take the baby far. And just the other day, after leaving Arden in the car with the babysitter so I could run into a shop, I was seized with the idea that something would happen to her. I ran as fast as I could for fear I would go back and find that she had been taken.

I have a wonderful babysitter whom I trust so much. Still, it freaks me out if she takes [the baby] to the park. It's one thing babysitting for me at my house. It's another thing taking her to the park. It scares me, but I don't want to put my fears on my baby.

—Odette

On the other hand, I can see a difference with how I parent my third child. I am able to do simple things that I was unable to do with Zachary because of my terror of separation and my inability to distinguish him as a person apart from myself and my childhood feelings. For example, I can leave Arden in the bedroom with the door closed while she sleeps. I was unable to do that with Zachary. I am able to go out more and leave the children with babysitters and enjoy my time away without calling every five minutes to make sure they are not only okay but still there.

Another way in which separation anxiety manifested itself was in the weaning of my three babies. The benefits of breastfeeding are inarguable, so I breastfed each one for more than a year. When it was time to wean Zachary (my first), I was shocked at the deep feelings of panic that came up for me. After talking with other adoptee mothers, though, it became clear that the fear of weaning was the fear of loss of connection, and loss of connection is like a death. Weaning the two younger children hasn't been much easier, but at least I have clarity about the feelings.

Recently, I had a revelation. I lay Arden down in bed, unable from sheer exhaustion to carry her any longer. She cried angrily that I had put her down, but as I watched her fight off the sleep she so desperately needed, I realized that letting her cry for a few moments didn't make me a bad mother. I was just a very tired mother, a mother still projecting my fears, my feelings of abandonment onto my baby. I sat next to her and whispered reassuring words and told her that I just couldn't keep carrying and rocking her, that I needed her to sleep. She fussed for a few moments, looked at me, and then fell asleep.

I have been unable to give her every part of me as I had her brother and sister, for that would take me away too much from the older children. That is the hardest part. I want to meet all their needs. I don't want them to feel left out, abandoned in any way. Yet how realistic is that? And how beneficial to them? I am scared I will mess my children up in some way, that I won't get it right. When I recently confessed my fears to my girlfriend, she replied, "Yes, you *will* screw up, and they will have some challenges themselves. Get over it!" We laughed.

My children are not me. My work as a mother is to respect them and allow them to be whoever they are, guide them, teach them, love them fully without holding back, kiss them as much as they will let me, hold them tight and then let them go. Day to day, I focus as much as I can on being in the present moment with my children. I try to remember, when I am not too exhausted and burned out, that life is fleeting, and soon they will grow and leave the nest. Some days this is not easy, especially when fear leads the way. But I can bring in faith and choose to see life differently. Today I feel wholeness, a sense of belonging, that I have never known before. I look into my children's eyes and they are familiar to me. It feels incredible. I love having a family!

I think of Jonathan before he met me, living on his own in our small two-bedroom house with all the space just for him. Now here we are, seven years later: Jonathan has a wife and three children, and most nights he sleeps in the lounge on Hot Wheels sheets with a Batman duvet (anywhere to get some sleep!). This is after his graduation from the top of a bunk bed while Zachary slept on the bottom (for a time, he needed Dad). Now Zachary and Kayla sleep in that room. Often they tiptoe into the lounge to climb into bed with Dad, or they scream for Mum (who is sleeping with the baby) and a cuddle. The most common words from our children at night are "Lie with me," or "Hold me!" Who can resist?

Changing Relationships

My two families have still not met and I have been in reunion now for sixteen years. The difference today is that we talk more about it. I am able to tell my adoptive family that I am going to visit my birth family without taking on their feelings. It is very freeing for me.

My relationships with both my adoptive family and my birth family are changing. I have less anger, I have more understanding, and the paradox is that finding my birth family has made me feel more a part of my adoptive family than ever before. They *are* my family and I truly love them. Our relationship today is better than it has ever been.

Pat recently called me about a TV show she had seen about daughters reuniting with their fathers. She told me she could hardly get her makeup on that morning because she was crying so much. She asked me whether she ought to write in to the show to see if they could help me locate my birth father. I said, "Yes!" Even though it's a long shot, anything is worth a try. This was the first time in the sixteen years of our reunion that Pat has offered to help me with my search. That willingness was what I wanted so much at the beginning of our reunion. But I have learned that healing takes time, and that gives me hope that all our relationships can continue to grow.

The hardest times are when my expectations are too high, when I want so badly for both families to understand me. I have learned the painful lesson that I am the only one who can identify and heal my wounds. Neither of my families can do that for me; they, too, have wounds that I cannot heal.

I am sure that as my own children grow, I will be faced with many challenges, both adoption-related and otherwise. I am both excited and daunted by it. Zachary just received a certificate for student of the month for creativity. He loves to make books on subjects that interest him, just like I did as a child. When he received his award, I was taken aback, not only by my motherly pride, but also by my emotions about it. Why should it be so strange to me that my child should love to write books, that Kayla and Arden love to sing and dance? I have done these things all my life. My children have become my reflection. I can finally look at myself in the mirror and know that I am not some unique, one-of-a-kind alien that landed on Earth with no explanation.

I belong, I am connected. I have a birth story, too.

RESOURCES

RECOMMENDED READING

I really urge you to read as much as you can; it is so helpful. The first adoption book I read was Nancy Verrier's *Primal Wound*. I was so amazed by her depth and clarity. I felt for the first time that someone really understood me. It was hard to read, and some days I would have to put it down and take a break from all the emotions that arose. But what a relief to know I wasn't the only one to feel the way I did! It all made so much sense once I understood adoption issues.

This is a list of adoption-related books. If you are searching or reunited, please take the time to read as many of them as you can. They will help you understand birthmothers, adoptees, and adoptive parents; as well as reunions and all the issues that go with adoption A lot of these books are available through your library or amazon.com.

Primal Wound, Nancy Verrier, MA
Eye-opening revelations of how separation at birth impacts adoptees lifelong.
http://www.nancyverrier.com

The Adoption Triangle, R. Pannor; A. Baran & Sorosky***
Learn about all sides of the adoption triangle.
Based on 1,000 interviews

Adoption Wisdom, Marlou Russell
http://www.marlourussellphd.com

Being Adopted: *The Lifelong Search for Self,*
Brodzinsky, Schecter and Henig

Birthright: *The Guide to Search and Reunion for Adoptees,*
Birthparents, and Adoptive Parents. Jean A. S. Strauss

Journey of the Adopted Self: *A Quest For Wholeness,*
Betty Jean Lifton***
Addresses the myths, fantasies, and skewed perceptions society and
many adoptive parents have about being adopted. One by one, the
author exposes the truths and realities of closed adoption as it
impacts adoptees.

Lost and Found, Betty Jean Lifton***
The adoption experience from primarily the adoptees's viewpoint.

The Other Mother, *A Woman's Love for the Child*
She Gave Up for Adoption, Carol Schaefer***

The Same Smile: *The Triumph of A Mother's Love*
After Losing Two Daughters
Susan Mello Souza
http://www.thesamesmile.com
mama_mazenga@thesamesmile.com

The Secret Life of the Unborn Child, Thomas Verney, M.D.*
What baby hears and senses in the last trimester of
pregnancy stays with him/her for life.

Twice Born, Betty Jean Lifton

Nobody's Child? Kasey Hamner
An adoptee's story from relinquishment through reunion.
http://www.kaseyhamner.com

25 Things Adopted Kids Wish Their Adoptive Parents Knew,
Sherrie Eldridge

Adoption Healing: A Path to Recovery, Joe Soll

Ghosts from the Nursery: Tracing the roots of violence
Robin Karr Morse and Meredith S. Wiley

Adoption and Loss: The Hidden Grief, Evelyn Burns Robinson
http://www.cloverpublications.com

*Available through:
"People Searching News" (PSN)
P.O. Box 100444
Palm Bay, FL 32910-0444

**Available through:
Concerned United Birthparents (CUB)
National Headquarters CUB, Inc.
2000 Walker Street
Des Moines, IA 50317

***Available through both PSN and CUB

WEBSITES

Here are some useful websites based in the both the US and in the UK. Special thanks to Alison Larkin for a comprehensive website. If you need a laugh, go to www.alisonlarkin.com - Alison is a comedian and the author of the award-winning show, *The English-American.*

Canadian Council of Natural Mothers
http://nebula.on.ca/canbmothers/

American Adoption Congress
Information on adoption reform. Great conferences and speakers.
http://www.americanadoptioncongress.org

National Adoption Information Clearinghouse:
Introduction to Search
http://www.calib.com/naic/adoptees/search.htm

Adopting.org: Especially for Adoptees
http://www.adopting.org/adoptees.html

RootsWeb's Guide to Tracing Family Trees:
Adoption and Orphans Research
http://www.rootsweb.com/ ~ rwguide/lesson31.htm

The Adoptees Internet Mailing List - http://www.aiml.org

Reunite.com - http://www.reunite.com

CUB - http://www.cubirthparents.org

United States-Based People & Organizations

If your geographical area is not listed, most of the organizations listed below will be able to refer you to someone close to home. Please note that phone numbers and addresses may change. If they have, call another number until you get someone who can help. If they don't call or email you back, *don't take it as a personal rejection!* Most of these organizations are run by overworked volunteers. Be persistent.

As for counselors, shop around. What works for one person may not work for another. If you don't gel with an individual counselor, find another one you do gel with.

CALIFORNIA
Los Angeles

Dr. Marlou Russell Ph.D. is the author of *Adoption Wisdom, a Guide to the Issues and Feelings of Adoption.* She is a highly respected psychologist in private practice in Santa Monica, California. Dr. Russell works with adoptees, birth parents, and adoptive families. She also speaks and writes on adoption issues for triad members, the public, and mental-health professionals. She is herself an adoptee in reunion with her birth family.
http://www.marlourussellphd.com

Adoption Care Services: Adoption-related support and workshops for parents-to-be, adoptive families, and all triad members.
http://www.AdoptionCareServices.com

San Francisco

Nancy Verrier, MA, author and individual counselor. Wrote
Primal Wound, widely considered one of the most illuminating
books about the long-term effects of adoption. Nancy is the mother
of two daughters—one who is adopted and one who is not—and an
advocate for children. She holds a master's degree in clinical
psychology and is in private practice in Lafayette, California. In
addition to her clinical and adoption work, Ms. Verrier writes and
lectures about the effects of early childhood trauma and deprivation
caused by premature separation from the mother under various
circumstances.
http://www.Nancyverrier.com

Ventura

Kids & Families Together offers a safe and supportive resource
center, where individuals, families, and the community can meet
and share information and concerns regarding foster, kinship, and
adoptive care.

670 Thompson Blvd.
Ventura CA 93001
Tel: (805) 643-1446
Fax: (805) 643-0271
http://www.kidsandfamilies.org

MASSACHUSETTS

Adoption Resource Center - The Center for Family Connections
An excellent, private, nonprofit organization dedicated to the
education and counseling of families blended by adoption, foster
care, guardianship, kinship, and divorce. Dr. Joyce Maguire Pavao,

author of *The Family of Adoption* (Beacon Press) has developed
models for therapy and training over twenty-five years

P.O. Box 383246,
Cambridge, MA 02238-3246
Tel: (617) 547-0909
Fax: (617) 497-5952

NEW MEXICO

Operation Identity - A support group for persons with adoption
connections
13101 Blackstone Road, NE
Albuquerque, NM 87122
Tel: (505) 293-3144

NEVADA

International Soundex Reunion Registry
PO Box 2312
Carson City, NV 89701-2312
(Include a self-addressed stamped envelope)

NEW YORK

Adoption Crossroads is the largest network of adoption search/
support groups with over 390 affiliates worldwide to help all those
affected by adoption. Referrals, reunion registry, counseling, online
bookstore, conferences, online articles, and a bulletin board for
posting adoption-related information.
http://www.adoptioncrossroads.org
Tel: (212) 988-0110

ALMA (Adoptees Liberty Movement Association)
A fully comprehensive search and support organization and registry
PO Box 727
Radio City Station
New York, NY 10101-0727
Tel: (212) 581-1568

CERA (Council on Equal Rights in Adoption)
401 East 74th Street
Suite 17D
New York, NY 10021
Tel: (212) 988-0110

Joe Soll, author and individual counselor, is an adoptee and author of *Adoptive Healing: A Path To Recovery*. He is also founder and director of Adoption Crossroads, a psychotherapist in private practice, a lecturer and former adjunct professor of social work at Fordham University Graduate School.

Joe Soll
74 Lakewood Drive
Congers NY 10920
Tel: (914) 286-0283

B. J. Lifton, author and individual adoption counselor. A pioneer in the adoption movement, whose book, *Lost and Found,* has become a bible to adoptees and to those who would understand the adoption experience. Ms Lifton has written three books in what has come to be known as the adoption trilogy: *Journey of the Adopted Self: A Quest for Wholeness*; *Lost and Found: The Adoption Experience*; and *Twice Born: Memoirs of An Adopted Daughter.* She also does adoption counseling with all members of the adoption triangle.

Betty Jean Lifton
BJKappa@aol.com

OHIO

Adoption Network Cleveland (ANC) is a nonprofit educational, support, advocacy and search organization for people affected by adoption. ANC operates an adoption helpline that receives over 2,600 calls a year, facilitates support-group meetings throughout Cuyahoga, Lorain, and Summit Counties, holds groups for adopted children and their parents, offers workshops for birthparents, families involved in open adoption, professionals and adult adoptees and birthparents in search. Founded in 1988, ANC has facilitated over 1,200 adoptee-birthparent reunions, and has been active in promoting legislation to open adoption records for adults. Members include adoptees, birthparents, adoptive parents, families and professionals who wish to openly explore adoption-related issues.

Adoption Network Cleveland
291 East 222nd Street
Cleveland, Ohio, 44123
Tel: (216) 261-1511
Fax: (216) 261-1164
http://www.adoptionetwork.org

UNITED KINGDOM-BASED WEBSITES AND ORGANIZATIONS

http://www.afteradoption.org.uk

Adoption About This site is full of articles written by young people who have a link with adoption, listing suggested reading and youth sites.
http://www.adoption.about.com

Adoption Excellence Institute is a bold, transatlantic collaboration between two independent adoption support organizations, After Adoption and the Center for Family Connections. The institute's mission is to help improve adoption practice worldwide, and will do this by stimulating discussion, collating research and providing a central point of access to research material.

http://www.bestofbothworlds.org

Adoptiontracker.com provides a free and unique internet-based service which tries to match the details of all its registrants with the details of those whom they are seeking.
http://www.adoptiontracker.com

Adoption UK provides support for adoptive families before, during and after adoption. They offer information and run a helpline (0800 7700 450 Mon-Fri 11am-4pm).

http://www.adoptionuk.org.uk

Birthlink runs the Contact Registry for Scotland and offers support, advice, and counseling.

birth.link@virgin.net

http://www.birthlink.org.uk

Telephone: 0131-225-6441 (Kate McDougal & Gary Clapton)

British Association for Adoption and Fostering (BAAF) is a leading membership organization for agencies and individuals concerned with adoption and fostering. The website holds the latest news on adoption reform, access to legislative documents, research reports, and publications.

http://www.baaf.org.uk

Fathers Direct - http://www.fathersdirect.com

Family Futures is a charity offering support and counseling for those who have suffered abuse or trauma in their family.

http://www.familyfutures.co.uk
lookupuk.com is a resource for finding lost friends or relatives.
http://www.lookupuk.com

Mothers Apart from Their Children -
http://www.matchmothers.org

**National Organization for the Counseling of Adoptees and
Parents** (NORCAP) provides advice and support to adopted people
and their birth relatives.
http://www.norcap.org.uk

Natural Parents Network (NPN) A national charity for natural
parents and relatives who have lost children to adoption.
http://www.n-p-n.fsnet.co.uk

NCH Action for Children provides a wide range of services
including family and community centers and special schools for over
16,000 children and young people.
http://www.nchafc.org.uk

NCH TALKadoption: If you live in the UK, have a link with
adoption, are under twenty-six years of age and want to talk, then
call the TALKadoption helpline free and in confidence.
Tel: 0808 808 1234 Mon - Fri 3 p.m. - 9 p.m.
http://www.talkadoption.org.uk

UK Birth-Adoption Register.Com is a resource for all adopted
people, birth parents and relatives wishing to contact one another.
There is a one-time registration fee of £10.00.
http://www.ukbirth-adoptionregister.com
http://www.adoptionregister.net
(a link to the Adoption Register web site)

For **birth certificates** apply to:

Public Search Room
St Catherine's House
10 Kingsway
London WC2B 6JB

The Registrar General
Adopted Children's Register
Titchfield
Fareham, Hants PO 15 5RV
(for England and Wales)

There are others for Scotland and Ireland but these places should be able to help you. Good luck!

(Footnotes)
* Written in 1086 by King William the Conqueror, *The Doomsday Book* was a survey of all the king's lands, including livestock, for the purpose of assessing taxes. It required two years to complete. Totteridge is listed at *Tattyrig*.
* My parents seemed unaware that my brother was abusing me until he went into a drug-treatment program.
* I have changed her name to protect her privacy.